TO

TIMOTHY DWIGHT

WHOSE INSTRUCTIONS IN BIBLICAL EXEGESIS AT THE YALE DIVINITY
SCHOOL ABIDE WITH ME AFTER THE LAPSE OF MORE THAN FORTY
YEARS AN INSPIRATION AND A DELIGHTFUL MEMORY

PREFACE.

MANY years of study in Christian doctrine have worked in me the conviction that the best method of conceiving and expounding the great truths of our holy religion is that which most accurately reproduces the ideas and teachings of the biblical writers. A scientific criticism of the books of the Old and New Testaments has prepared the way for a clearer and more thoroughgoing apprehension of their doctrinal contents, and has brought about a reasonable recognition of the progress of doctrine traceable in both Testaments. The conspicuous human element in the Scriptures is no longer so universally ignored as in former years, and students of the Bible are everywhere disposed to recognize the varieties of thought and style among the prophets, evangelists, and apostles.

One has only to look into the old catechisms and text-books of dogmatic theology to perceive how much the modern Church has been accustomed to accept without question from mediæval and early Protestant scholasticism. Writers on Christian doctrine were once accustomed to cite their proof-texts at random from poet and chronicler, patriarch and apostle. So long as it was "in the Bible," it mattered not with the polemical dogmatist whether the text adduced were a "Verily, verily" of Jesus Christ, or an utterance of "Elihu the son of Barachel the Buzite, of the family of Ram," when "his wrath was kindled against Job," or a fragment from "the words of King Lemuel, which his mother taught him."

It has taken more than a hundred years of reaction against such an irrational use of the Holy Scriptures to bring to the front the more sober and scientific methods of biblical theology which prevail to-day among the influential students and theologians of Christendom. But as is usual in such reactions the leaders of the movement have been too generally men of a rationalistic and iconoclastic spirit. For long time their labors made but little advance against the current methods and the dominant systems of religious teaching, and even at the present time it is matter of remark that a large proportion of the American clergy have no intelligent appreciation of the vast amount of work that has been accomplished toward the reconstruction of doctrinal systems by means of a more thorough exposition of the Scriptures. It is, however, coming to be seen more and more that even rationalistic and iconoclastic writers may indirectly serve the cause of truth. If they but stimulate the lover of God's truth to revise his unscientific methods, to forsake untenable theories, and to build more wisely and securely, their very extravagance may prove a help to us. We may profit much by their skillful labors of minute research, though we reject much of what they think to be of value. And so we may repeat what Hurst wrote nearly forty years ago: "A glance at the various departments of theology which have received most attention within the last half century will prove that rationalism has been the undesigned means of contributing to their advancement. The faith of the public teacher determines the faith and practice of the masses; and those who are the commissioned expounders of truth for the

THE MEDIATION
OF
JESUS CHRIST

A Contribution to the Study of
Biblical Dogmatics

BY
MILTON S. TERRY, D.D., LL.D.
Professor in Garrett Biblical Institute

There is one God, one Mediator also between God and men,
himself man, Christ Jesus, who gave
himself a Ransom for all

Wipf & Stock
PUBLISHERS
Eugene, Oregon

Wipf and Stock Publishers
199 W 8th Ave, Suite 3
Eugene, OR 97401

The Mediation of Jesus Christ
A Contribution to the Study of Biblical Dogmatics
By Terry, Milton S.
ISBN: 1-59752-113-2
Publication date 3/8/2005
Previously published by Eaton and Mains, 1903

people have to-day a more substantial basis of theological literature than their predecessors possessed before rationalism appeared in Germany."[1]

In the following pages I have made an attempt to set forth the scriptural doctrine of Christ's redemptive MEDIATION. The title I have chosen for the book is preferred to Atonement, Reconciliation, Redemption, and other terms of like import, as being on the whole more comprehensively expressive of the ever-living presence and power of our Lord as the Saviour of mankind. Our theological libraries are stocked with "works on the Atonement," and it would be presumptuous to add another unless it show something in content, scope, or method sufficient to justify a new treatise on an old and familiar theme. Our apology is that in the standard literature on this subject one has to look over many a volume before he will find a work that is not largely given to a discussion of the divers theories and polemic issues of the past, or else is notably defective in handling the scriptural teaching. There seems to be ample room for a book of moderate size which shall confine itself to a faithful exposition of what the biblical writers tell us concerning the mediatorial revelation and ministry of Jesus Christ.

In speaking as we do of the comparative lack of works giving a noticeably biblical treatment of Christ's mediation, we mean no disparagement of those able discussions of the Atonement which have commanded deserved attention, and have shed light upon the nature, the necessity, the sufficiency, and the extent of the saving work of Jesus. There are many minds that take hold of great truths best when they see them set in

---

[1] *History of Rationalism*, pp. 579, 580. New York, 1865. The same statement may be repeated to-day with even greater assurance than in 1865.

systematic and logical forms of thoughtful disquisition, and such minds are often repelled by the details of biblical criticism and exegesis, for which they have no taste and with which they have little patience. Moreover, a discussion of the atonement in Christ may be in complete accord with scriptural teaching and yet be conspicuously nonbiblical in its method.

It will be noticed by some that the method of this book is substantially the same as that followed in my little volume on *The New and Living Way,* which was published about a year ago. Both these discussions are in fact fragments of a larger treatise which has been slowly growing in my hands for many years, and which I hope to publish at some future day. The aim throughout is to furnish the reader with a purely scriptural presentation of "God in Christ reconciling the world unto himself." In the present volume I have perhaps made a slight departure from the biblical method in my second chapter, where a brief notice is taken of the ideals of incarnation traceable among the various nations. But even this exception is so in touch with biblical conceptions of incarnate mediation that no reader, we hope, will find fault with our calling attention to the interesting facts, and our supplying in footnotes a few references to the sources from which our statements have been derived, and where further information may be found.

Except in occasional footnotes, the reader will find in this volume scarcely a reference to the polemical issues and methods of the older dogmatics. This omission arises from no lack of appreciation of our rich inheritance from the past. But those who are concerned with the former controversies may find them set forth in superabundance in the works on systematic theology, and in numerous special treatises on the

PREFACE.   9

Atonement. I offer no other apology for my course of procedure than the contents and methods of the book itself. So far as the essential facts of Christ's mediation are to be noted, and the nature, necessity, purpose, reason, sufficiency, and extent of the redemption that is in him are to receive attention in the following pages, the reader must look to find them discussed in connection with those scriptures where they are believed to be expressed or recognized. We do not treat them as just so many distinctive propositions to be maintained, but rather as facts and teachings of the biblical record to be fairly expounded, each in the light of its own context.

We append to this volume a bibliography, which, aside from its main purpose as a help for special students, may also help ordinary readers to see how long and laborious has been the task of bringing biblical theology into the prominence it holds to-day. Our list is far from complete, and aims only to present a select but reasonably full catalogue of works in the department of doctrine to which this little volume belongs. Few of all the books named in the list can be unqualifiedly indorsed, but they are all needful for understanding the history and trend of modern theology, so far as modern thought recognizes the Bible as in any sense a norm of doctrine. The value of this body of literature may be inferred from the following statements of Beyschlag, found in the Introduction to his *New Testament Theology:*

> The presupposition that the Bible must everywhere teach with the same divine perfection caused the Church to fall into the most arbitrary allegorical exposition, and in spite of appeals to Holy Scripture made the Church's doctrine more and more unlike the announcement of salvation which Scripture contains. The Reformation went back in earnest to the Scriptures, but it suffered so much of that

erroneous assumption to remain as might render a more biblical dogmatic possible, but not an historical knowledge of the doctrinal contents of the Bible. And the rigidity of the Protestant system soon led back to a new scholasticism, which again closed the Bible that had scarcely been opened. It was therefore reserved for the time of the decay of this Protestant scholasticism, and the beginning of the critical and historical study of the Bible, to advance gradually to the idea of a biblical theology as now understood. Genuine friends of orthodoxy were the first, from the sense of the insufficiency and obsoleteness of its scholastic form, to endeavor to regenerate it from the utterly neglected Bible, and thus did the name *Biblical Theology*—in the sense of a biblical as distinguished from a scholastic dogmatic—first become current in the latter part of the eighteenth century.

CONTENTS AND ANALYTICAL OUTLINE.

CHAPTER I.

THE MYSTERY AND PURPOSE OF THE AGES.

	PAGE
1. Christ a Revelation of God	15
2. All Grace and Truth from God	16
3. God's Mystery and Purpose	17
4. "Promised before Times Eternal"	18
5. Accords with Highest Teleology	19

CHAPTER II.

THE DOCTRINE AND IDEALS OF INCARNATION.

1. Johannine Concept of the Incarnation	20
2. Self-revelation of God a Process through Ages	21
3. Revelation Cosmical and Personal	21
4. Man the Image of God	22
5. Chinese and Mazdian Ideas	23
6. Hindu Avatars	24
7. Ideas of Incarnation in Brahmanism	24
8. Doctrine of Transmigration	25
9. Buddhist Ideas of Incarnation	26
10. Older Ideas of the Vedic Hymns	26
(1) Varuna. (2) Indra. (3) Agni	27, 28
11. Egyptian Ideas of Incarnation	29
12. Greek Ideas of Deity	31
13. Corresponding Ideas of the Latin Mythology	31
14. Idea of God not Evolved by Reasoning	32
15. Biblical Anthropomorphism	33
16. God's Immanence in all the World	34
17. Not without Witness among all the Nations	35
18. Incarnation of Christ the Supreme Revelation of God	37

CHAPTER III.

IDEAS OF MEDIATION SYMBOLIZED IN PRIESTLY SERVICE AND IN THE LEVITICAL RITUAL.

1. Primitive Ideas of Priesthood and Mediation	38
2. Moses and Samuel as Priestly Mediators	39
3. The Levitical Priesthood	40
4. Significance of Levitical Mediation	41

CONTENTS.

	PAGE
5. The Sacrificial Offerings	42
(1) Cereal Offerings	43
(2) Burnt Offerings	44
(3) Peace Offerings	44
(4) Trespass Offerings	45
(5) The Sin Offering	46
(6) Day of Atonement	46
(7) The Goat for Azazel	47
6. Symbolical Significance of Blood Offered in Sacrifice	48
7. The Consuming of the Flesh	49
8. Meaning of the Word כפר and its Derivatives	50
9. Force of Sacrificial Allusions	51
10. Priesthood and Sacrifice Express Deep Religious Convictions	52
11. Typical of Christ's Perfect Mediation	53
12. Erroneous Notions of the Offering of Blood to God	54

CHAPTER IV.

IDEAS OF MEDIATION IN THE PROPHETS AND THE PSALMS.

1. A Deeper Spiritual View of Approaching God	55
2. The Teaching of Hosea, Isaiah, and Jeremiah	56
3. The Import of Isa. lii, 13, to liii, 12	58
4. The Penitential Psalms	61
5. Import of Psa. xxii	62
6. Connection of These with Israel's Messianic Hope	64
7. Significance of Dan. ix, 24	65

CHAPTER V.

DOCTRINE OF JESUS IN THE SYNOPTIC GOSPELS.

1. Relative Importance of Jesus's Words	67
2. His "Life a Ransom for Many"	68
(1) Significance of the Word λύτρον	68
(2) Christ's Entire Life Given as a Ransom	70
(3) Remote Analogies to be Ignored	71
3. Words of Jesus at the Last Supper	72

CHAPTER VI.

DOCTRINE OF JESUS IN THE FOURTH GOSPEL.

1. Peculiarities of John's Gospel	77
2. Confirms and Supplements the Synoptics	78
3. Doctrine of John iii, 14-16	78
4. His Flesh and Blood Given for the Life of the World	80
5. Dying for Others	81
6. Intercessory Prayer in Chapter xvii	82
7. Scope of Gospels not to Teach Significance of Jesus's Death	84

CONTENTS. 13

CHAPTER VII.

DOCTRINE OF THE OTHER JOHANNINE WRITINGS.

	PAGE
1. Doctrine of the First Epistle	85
2. Use of Old Testament Imagery of Blood Offerings	87
3. A Living Advocate with the Father	88
4. Coming "through Water and Blood"	89
5. Testimony of the Spirit	92
6. Doctrine of the Apocalypse	93

CHAPTER VIII.

DOCTRINE OF PETER.

1. Peter's Discourses in the Acts of the Apostles	95
2. Teaching of the First Epistle	96
3. Partaking in Christ's Sufferings	98

CHAPTER IX.

DOCTRINE OF THE PAULINE EPISTLES.

1. Paul's Discourses in the Acts of the Apostles	100
2. The Corinthian Epistles	100
(1) 2 Cor. v, 14-19	101
(2) The Reconciliation unto God	102
(3) God Originates, Christ Mediates, the Reconciliation	106
(4) 2 Cor. v, 21: "Sin for Us"	107
3. Epistle to the Galatians	108
(1) Gal. iii, 13: "A Curse for Us"	108
(2) Gal. iv, 4	111
(3) Gal. ii, 19, 20	111
4. Epistle to the Romans	112
(1) Rom. iii, 21-26. Six Points of Note	112
(2) Rom. iv, 25. Continual Work of Reconciliation	129
(3) Rom. v, 12-21. The Great Antithesis	131
5. Epistles to Ephesians and Colossians	132
6. The Pastoral Epistles	134

CHAPTER X.

DOCTRINE OF THE EPISTLE TO THE HEBREWS.

1. Outline of the Epistle	136
2. Large Use of Old Testament in the Epistle	137
3. Superior Priesthood of Jesus	138
4. "After the Order of Melchizedek"	138
5. Symbolism of the Tabernacle	139
6. Offered Once for All	140

CONTENTS.

7. Heb. ix, 15–18. "Testament" or "Covenant"?...... 141
   (1) Reasons for "Testament".................... 142
   (2) Reasons for "Covenant"..................... 143
   (3) Covenants "over Dead Victims".............. 147
   (4) This Covenant not between Equals........... 149
8. Uniqueness of the Epistle......................... 150
9. Substantial Agreement of all the New Testament Writers 151

CHAPTER XI.

CHRIST'S MEDIATION EFFICIENT THROUGH THE SPIRIT.

1. Departure of Christ Expedient..................... 152
2. Significance of the Word "Comforter"............. 153
3. Procession and Personality of the Spirit............. 154
4. "The Spirit of God"............................. 155
5. The Spirit One with God.......................... 156
6. Three Fundamental Truths Concerning the Spirit..... 158
7. Mediation Consequently Ever Continuous........... 160
8. "The Seven Spirits before the Throne"............. 160
9. Operations of the Holy Spirit...................... 161
   (1) Conviction of Sin, Righteousness, and Judgment. 162
   (2) Regeneration............................... 166
   (3) Sanctification.............................. 167
   (4) Witness and Communion..................... 169
   (5) Revealing the Truth......................... 170
   (6) Imparting Gifts of Power.................... 172
   (7) The Comforter.............................. 175
10. Through These Operations God in Christ Reconciles the World... 176

CHAPTER XII.

SUMMARY OF THE BIBLICAL DOCTRINE.

1. Mediation a Continuous Process, not a Finished Work. 177
2. Largely Set Forth by Symbols and Metaphors........ 178
3. Use by Christ and Apostles of Current Forms of Speech 180
4. Necessity of Christ's Mediation..................... 181
   (1) A Necessity in Man......................... 182
   (2) A Necessity in the Nature of God............. 183
5. Such Suffering not Penal........................... 184
6. Does not Remove all Consequences of Sin........... 185
7. Not an Objective Process Outside of Humanity....... 185
8. Christ's Mediation Essentially Spiritual............. 186
9. Effectual through a Living Faith.................... 187
10. No Theory of Atonement Sufficient to Explain all the Facts of Christ's Mediation....................... 188
11. The Mystical Body of Christ Made One with God..... 190

THE MEDIATION OF JESUS CHRIST.

CHAPTER I.

THE MYSTERY AND PURPOSE OF THE AGES.

FROM a New Testament point of view it appears that all the mysterious problems of the moral world center in Jesus Christ and must find their final solution in the manifestation of his person, his mediatorial activity, and the coming of his kingdom. For according to these Scriptures the Lord Jesus is a revelation of the invisible God. One of his most re- *Christ a revelation* markable sayings is, "All things have *of God.* been delivered unto me of my Father: and no one knoweth the Son, save the Father; neither doth any know the Father, save the Son, and he to whomsoever the Son willeth to reveal him" (Matt. xi, 27). Whatever other ideas we derive from the prologue of John's Gospel, this one thought is clear beyond controversy, that all saving grace and truth spring from the bosom of God. This entire Gospel is pre- *Grace and truth* eminently a record of God's revelation *from God.* of himself through incarnation in the person of his "only begotten Son," and the opening words of the First Epistle of John, written obviously by the same author, are a noteworthy comment on the statements of the Gospel, and a confirmation of them: "That which was from the beginning, that which we have heard, that which we have seen with our eyes, that which we beheld, and our hands handled, concerning the Word of life (and the life was manifested, and we have seen, and bear witness, and declare unto you the life, the eternal life, which was with the Father, and was manifested unto us), that which we have seen and heard declare we unto you also, that ye also may have fellowship with us." The language and style of this writer bear the peculiar marks of a devout mysticism, but we recognize in his various statements the testimony of a most real and vivid experience. He is no dreaming mystic that cannot distinguish between facts and fancies. He knows by unmistakable acquaintance "that Jesus Christ is come in the flesh," and he desires that others partake with him in the hallowed fellowship and joy. It was a saying of one of the early Christian fathers that the beloved disciple John had leaned so much upon his Master's bosom that he himself became almost another Jesus.

This revelation of God in Christ is often spoken of, especially in the writings of Paul, as a holy "mystery" (μυστήριον). In the twenty-seven passages of the Greek Testament in which this word occurs it always denotes some blessed spiritual truth, some hidden fact or mystical relation, which, though withheld from the

GOD'S MYSTERY AND PURPOSE. 17

many who care for none of these things, is made known to them that have the Spirit of God. God's mystery and 1 Cor. ii, 7, Paul speaks of "God's wis- purpose. dom in a mystery, that which has been hidden, which God foreordained before the ages unto our glory." In Rom. viii, 28-30, he teaches that the calling, justification, and glorification of those who are "conformed to the image of his Son" are but the foreseen and ordained steps of a well-defined purpose of God. In Rom. ix, 11, he mentions "the purpose of God according to election" in the relations of Jacob and Esau, and in the doxology with which that epistle closes we read of "the revelation of the mystery which hath been kept in silence through times eternal, but now is manifested, and through the Scriptures of the prophets, according to the commandment of the eternal God, is made known unto all nations unto obedience of faith" (Rom. xvi, 25, 26). In Eph. i, 9-11, we read of "the mystery of his will, according to the good pleasure which he purposed in him unto a dispensation of the fullness of the times, to sum up all things in Christ, the things in the heavens and the things upon the earth; even in him in whom also we were made a heritage, having been foreordained according to the purpose of him who worketh all things after the counsel of his will."[1] The same

---

[1] It is no help to an understanding of this purpose and mystery of the ages to complicate it with the conception of a "covenant between the Father and the Son" as the basis of human redemption, or to impose upon our theology the doctrines of "the covenant of works" and "the covenant of grace," after the manner of the so-called "Federal Theology." The postulates of such theology belong to the speculative and scholastic methods of the

2

18   THE MEDIATION OF JESUS CHRIST.

idea finds repeated statement in Eph. iii, 9, 11, and in Col. i, 26. It appears also in Titus i, 1-3, where eternal life is spoken of as a boon "which God, who cannot lie, promised before times eternal." The word "promised" here suggests a vivid conception in the writer's mind of the ancient promises recorded in the Hebrew Scriptures, yet so associated in common thought with God's eternal purpose of grace that promise and purpose are scarcely distinguished from each other. Also in 2 Tim. i, 9, 10, salvation and the holy calling accord with God's "own purpose and grace, which was given us in Christ Jesus before times eternal, but hath now been manifested by the appearing of our Saviour Christ Jesus." Here the word "given," like "promised," in Titus i, 2, is expressive of something purposed in eternity, but realized in time. So, too, in 1 Pet. i, 20, Christ is conceived "as a lamb without blemish and without spot, who was foreknown indeed before the foundation of the world, but was manifested at the end of the times."[1]

---

sixteenth and seventeenth centuries, and have no legitimate place in modern biblical dogmatics. The figure of a covenant between God and Noah, and God and Abraham, and God and Israel, is sufficiently familiar; and the doctrine of Christ as mediator of the new covenant of God with a new Israel is to be duly recognized in its proper connection. But the figure of a covenant, compact, stipulation, or agreement between God and Christ, whatever truth it may contain, is too far removed from the direct scriptural testimony to require formal discussion in these pages.

[1] Stevens observes that in emphasizing the divine purpose Paul "shared that intense and living sense of God and of his causal efficiency which was characteristic of the Hebrew mind. God's action is the expression of his purpose. The work of salvation is the realization of a gracious plan which lay in the mind of God before the world was. Sometimes the divine purpose is conceived

GOD'S MYSTERY AND PURPOSE. 19

Whatever, therefore, we make of Christ's redeeming work, we must recognize its origin in the bosom of God, the everlasting Father, and conceive it both as a holy mystery and as an eternal purpose of love and wisdom, developing through untold ages. This sublime conception accords notably with all that is highest and best in the theistic doctrines of teleology. The universe of being shows manifold evidences of intelligent design. Back of all phenomena exists not only an invisible Force in which all things consist and hold together, but also a supreme Intelligence, which sees the end of all things from their beginning. We see but parts of his ways, and may therefore often fall into error in our efforts to point out the design and to unfold the mysteries of the high and holy One who inhabiteth eternity; but we do well to give heed to the teachings of prophets and apostles, and especially to everything connected with the manifestation of Jesus Christ; for in him and through him are we most likely to obtain our deepest knowledge, both of the mysteries and the purposes of God.

Accords with highest teleology.

---

of as eternal; sometimes as historical. In either case the treatment of the subject is not speculative, but practical and religious. The references to God's purpose illustrate the effort to form a rational conception of God's historic action, to find an ideal principle underlying the course of the world, and to correlate the doctrines of the Gospel with the character of God. For Paul the purposes of God are rooted in the nature of God."—*Theology of the New Testament,* p. 376. New York, 1899.

CHAPTER II.

THE DOCTRINE AND IDEALS OF INCARNATION.

THE doctrine of John's Gospel is that the WORD, in whom was the life and the light of men, was in the beginning with God, and in some inexplicable manner was God, became flesh, and dwelt (ἐσκήνωσεν, *abode as in a tabernacle*) among us. We recognize in this allusion an ideal derived from Exod. xl, 34-38, where it is said that the glory of Jehovah filled the tabernacle and hung like a luminous cloud above that sacred dwelling "in the sight of all the house of Israel, throughout all their journeys;" for the writer of the Gospel immediately adds: "We beheld his glory, glory as of an only begotten from a father;" and in verse 18 he says that "no man hath seen God at any time; the only begotten Son, who is in the bosom of the Father, he has declared him." Here is a very remarkable presentation of the doctrine of divine incarnation, and it would seem from the teachings both of John and of Paul that the great purpose of the ages, hidden from times eternal but disclosed through the manifestation and the mediation of Christ, was a marvelous INCARNATION OF DEITY.

The doctrine of the mediation of Jesus Christ cannot receive a full scriptural exposition apart from that of incarnation. "God was in Christ reconciling the world

GOD'S SELF-REVELATION A PROCESS.   21

unto himself," and as this reconciliation was the purpose and the mystery of the ages we should think of it as a process carried on through the ages. These ages have their epochs and crises and consummations. The regeneration and spiritual elevation of mankind are not effected in a moment of time, nor are human hearts, with all their emotions and intelligence, the creation of an instantaneous act of omnipotence. A human spirit, possessed of intellect, feelings, and the freedom of moral action, is not changed from darkness to light or from light to darkness by any sudden and arbitrary exercise of divine power. In accordance with these facts we shall find that the self-revelation of God is a process running through ages and generations.

<small>God's self-revelation a process through ages.</small>

The great truths of incarnation may be shown to have had from the beginning both cosmical and personal expression in many different ways. "The divers portions and divers manners" (Heb. i, 1) of God's outward expression of "his everlasting power and divinity" (Rom. i, 20) may be traced in manifold phenomena to which it has not always occurred to man to apply a spiritual interpretation. There has been a vast deal of "searching after God," but too little attention to the fact that God has been always seeking to make his nature known to man. The heavens have declared his glory, and the visible wonders of his creation have made known his power and his wisdom, but the vain reasonings and senseless hearts of men have too generally perverted the

<small>Revelation cosmical and personal.</small>

heavenly Father's disclosures of his goodness (comp. Rom. i, 19-23). Before we pass to the more direct biblical teaching we may well point out some facts which go to show that God has been revealing himself unto all the peoples in their divers concepts of the incarnation of Deity. The myths, the vague conjectures, and even some of the strange superstitions of the heathen world may serve to indicate how the most ancient tribes of men had concepts of divine revelation and incarnation written in their hearts.

It is maintained by some writers that the idea of incarnation is a part of the crude beliefs of rude society in its earliest stages. God is always conceived, they tell us, as essentially human in those early cults, but later and more accurate thinking brings about the conviction of an impassable gulf between God and man.[1] But we may boldly challenge this assumption, and submit as a more trustworthy opinion that this human way of thinking about God is a very proper conception. The heavenly Father may naturally be believed to be very much like his noblest offspring, and the alleged "impassable gulf which later thought opens out between them" is an erroneous fancy

Man the image of God.

---

[1] Thus J. G. Frazer: "The notion of a man-god, or of a human being endowed with divine or supernatural powers, belongs essentially to that earlier period of religious history in which gods and men are still viewed as beings of much the same order. . . . Strange, therefore, as may seem to us the idea of a god incarnate in human form, it has nothing very startling for early man, who sees in a man-god or a god-man only a higher degree of the same supernatural powers which he arrogates in perfect good faith to himself. Such incarnate gods are common in rude society."—*The Golden Bough*, vol. i, p. 32. London, 1894.

IDEALS OF INCARNATION.   23

of deistic speculation. The biblical doctrine, and a view to our thought much more truthful, is that man is in fact the highest visible image and likeness of the invisible God, and that the various ideals of incarnation traceable in the religious thought and the mythologies of the nations are so many evidences of the loving "Father of the spirits of all flesh" making himself known to his human offspring.

We are informed that the ancient Chinese fathers employed a primitive written character as a visible symbol of the idea of *manifestation*, or revelation, thereby expressing their belief in a real communication between Heaven and men.[1] In the Zoroastrian scriptures we read of the Iranian sage receiving revelations through the archangel Vohuman, who showed himself to him in colossal form, "nine times as large as a man," and conducted him "in ecstatic trance into the glorious and dazzling presence of Ahura-Mazda and the Amshaspands," where he was instructed in the doctrines of the Mazdian faith.[2]

Chinese and Mazdian ideas.

---

[1] See James Legge, *The Religions of China*, p. 11. London, 1880.
[2] Jackson, *Zoroaster, the Prophet of Ancient Iran*, pp. 40-42. New York, 1899. In the *Dinkart*, book v, chap. ii, it is said that Zoroaster "was spiritually fashioned in the pure light, and provided undefectively for the acceptance and propagation of the religion in the world. And when he is sent for the manifestation of restrained saintliness and bodily substance great glory and radiance become discernible in him." Elsewhere it is written that "the coming of the religion at a given time resembles the birth of a child through two united powers. . . . The religion of the Mazda-worshipers became manifest on the earth like the reception of a child by mothers and delivering it back to the fathers." See *Sacred Books of the East*, vol. xlvii, pp. 122, 133, 134.

Hindu mythology is particularly noted for its innumerable stories of incarnation, which are called

Hindu avatars. avatars, or descents of the various deities. The god Vishnu is remarkable for his many manifestations. Whenever iniquity seems to triumph and religion is exposed to danger he issues forth from the unseen in some new avatar.[1] Some of these Hindu incarnations bear a very mystical character, and resemble the "emanations" of gnosticism, as being essentially outflowings of the divine substance. These, however, belong rather to the refined speculations of oriental theosophy.[2]

But back of all these avatars of the later Hinduism we find an older cult, in which Brahm is conceived as

Brahmanism. the divine spiritual essence from which all things proceed, and Brahma is his first manifestation, as the supreme Creator, the first lawgiver of the Indian race, and the inspirer of the ancient Vedas. The priests of this cult are called by way of preeminence the Brahmans; they are said to have sprung from the head of Brahma; they form the highest caste of India, and their persons are regarded

---

[1] So in the *Bhagavad Gita* (iv, 7, 8) he says, "I manifest myself from age to age for the defense of the good, for the suppression of the wicked, and for the establishment of justice."

[2] "An *avatara*," says Barth, "in the highest and fullest sense of the word, is not a transitory manifestation of the deity, still less the procreation, by the connection of a god with a mortal, of a being in some sense intermediate; it is the presence, at once mystic and real, of the Supreme Being in a human individual, who is both truly god and truly man, and this intimate union of the two natures is conceived of as surviving the death of the individual in whom it was realized."—*The Religions of India,* p. 170. Trans. by Wood. Boston, 1882.

DOCTRINE OF REINCARNATION.

as sacred and inviolable. Along with divers philosophical conceptions of the origin of all things, there appears also a pantheistic doctrine of the soul of the world, an original principle (*atman, self*) capable of assuming all manner of visible forms and of effecting all the changes that occur in the universe.

The doctrine of "transmigration," or reincarnation, is conspicuous in all the native religions of India. The human soul is thought of as some subtle, incomprehensible principle of life which is brought down into narrow limitations by attachment to the changing world. Swept into the vortex of human ways of life, it becomes ignorant of its true nature, seeks sensual gratification, and sinks lower and lower. Rebirth is a form of punishment imposed upon the groveling soul until it turns to know itself, and when it learns that it is one in essence with the great soul of the world, and shapes its life and thought accordingly, it attains deliverance from all evil desires and absorption into the primal essence. Herein Brahmanism and Buddhism are at one. The ultimate goal of all human incarnation and struggle is the "Nirvana" of union and identity with the Infinite, the Universal, the Absolute.

<small>Transmigration.</small>

Buddhism itself presents to us a very remarkable idea of incarnation. It is peculiar in that it recognizes no supreme Being, who is self-existent and eternal, and so it breaks away from the older Brahmanism. In fact, it seems to deny the real existence of any incorporeal spirit, whether

<small>Buddhism.</small>

human or divine. But one fundamental tenet of this system is that the so-called Buddhas are beings who repeatedly make their appearance in human form, yet only after immense intervals of time. Previous to his incarnation in human form the Buddha is believed to have passed through various phases of manifestation, at one time appearing as a reptile, at another as a bird; but when at last he appears as Buddha he is always born of a woman, and born under the ordinary laws of human life. The distinguishing characteristics of the Buddha, as at once an incarnation and a manifestation of the highest excellence, are calmness, gentleness, and repose. Here we perceive an ideal of all that is noblest and best in moral attainment set forth before us in the form of a perfected human being.[1]

But we must go back of Buddhism and Brahmanism to the hymns of the most ancient Veda to find the

Ideas in the Vedic hymns. earliest religious conceptions of the ancestors of the tribes of India. Popular songs usually embody portraitures of the common

---

[1] "Gautama Buddha himself was merely the last link in a long chain of corporeal forms, and he had been preceded by twenty-four Buddhas, who were to previous ages of the world what he was to the present. Every one of these Buddhas was gifted with the faculty of recollecting his previous personalities, and Gautama often gave an account of his own former existences."—Monier-Williams, *Buddhism, in Its Connection with Brahmanism and Hinduism, and in Its Contrast with Christianity,* p. 111. London, 1889. Bishop Copleston observes: "The qualities most charming to the Indian mind are gentleness and calm. . . . The picture which is given to us of Gotama represents a character not only calm and gentle, but active, genial, not devoid of humor, deeply sympathetic, and intensely human."—*Buddhism Primitive and Present in Magadha and in Ceylon,* p. 97. London, 1892. See also R. Spence Hardy, *Eastern Monachism,* pp. 3-5. London, 1860.

IDEALS IN THE VEDIC HYMNS. 27

life and thoughts of their time, and numerous hymns of the Rig-Veda carry us back to the time when the old Aryans entered India through those same northwestern passes by which Alexander led his victorious forces some two thousand years afterward. The Indus and the rivers of the Punjab water the fair fields where the action of the Vedas is laid, and these old poems show us that their authors conceived all the visible forms and the forces of nature as instinct with Deity, and as so many objects of worship. Out of this general conception it was possible to form various divergent ideas of God, and we do, in fact, find some Vedic hymns clearly polytheistic in doctrine, others which are pantheistic, and some which seem to breathe a pure monotheism. The term *henotheism* was employed by Max Müller to denote the worship often represented in the hymns in which the Deity addressed appears to be for the time the only God recognized by the worshiper.

Highest and central among the Vedic deities is Varuna, identical with the Greek Ouranos. He is the all-embracing Heaven, the former and ruler of all things. The sun in the heavens, the moon and the stars in their courses, the seasons in their rounds are his appointments. He numbers the winkings of each mortal eye, and observes all that is hidden in the secret places of the world. The counsels of human hearts are open before him.

<small>Varuna.</small>

Other hymns address Indra as the god of the clear

blue sky, the air-space, whence come fertilizing rains,
without which the people of northwestern India are quickly reduced to general suffering. The language of these Indra hymns is remarkably forcible and simple of comprehension to those who have lived some time in India and have watched there the phenomena of the changing seasons. These hymns accord with ideals of an ancient nature-myth. The clouds are conceived as the covering of hostile demons, who hide the sun from view, darken the world, and hold back the heavenly waters from the thirsty earth. It is the glory of Indra that he alone can vanquish the dreadful demons. Other gods shrink back from the roaring monsters, but Indra boldly goes forth to meet them, armed with his fatal thunderbolt; he smites them with his rapid lightnings, pierces their covering of clouds, and releases the waters, which thereupon fall at once in copious showers to bless the earth.

Indra.

The principal earth-god, to whom more hymns are addressed than to any other, is Agni (Latin *ignis*), the god of fire. His proper home is heaven, but he has come as representative of other gods to bring light and comfort to the dwellings of men. His births are without number, for he appears every day in various forms of life. He lies concealed in the soft wood, and when two sticks are rubbed together Agni springs forth in gleaming brightness. He is also born of the floods of heaven, and comes down in the form of lightning to the earth.

Agni.

EGYPTIAN MYTHS.   29

In fact, he is a kind of priest both in heaven and upon earth. He goes forth wisely as a messenger and mediator between gods and men; and when the sun goes down, and darkness covers the earth, the kindled fire and light proclaim that Agni is mightier than all the spirits of darkness.

We need not refer to other deities of the Vedic pantheon, for the conceptions which attach to the above-named suffice to show how even nature-myths evince the doctrine of incarnation. The all-embracing heaven, the moving elements and the forces of earth and sky and air, are full of God. The mythical pictures of Agni are but a poetic clothing of beneficent fire and light in such apparent forms as will enable them to dwell with men and so manifest the riches of the grace of the heavenly Power.

The ancient religion of the Egyptians is so veiled in mystery that it is next to impossible to determine the real elements of its earliest forms. It has been denied that the old Egyptian creed gives any evidence of the idea of incarnation,[1] but the fact that so many of the Egyptian deities *Egyptian ideas*

---

[1] Hardwick thinks that man's relation to God as offspring and as bearing the divine image was very faint in the Egyptian cult, and he observes that in accord with "this lack of faith in the harmonious meeting of the human and divine is the remarkable absence from the old Egyptian creed of the idea of incarnation."— *Christ and Other Masters*, p. 511. Fourth ed., London, 1875. But there is room for doubting the correctness of this statement. The creed which is studied in existing texts taken from the pyramids seems at best but a confused evolution out of diverse prehistoric faiths and local cults, and Erman says: "Like the Greeks, the Egyptians allowed their imagination to weave all manner of legends round the gods, and to remodel their shapeless great

are depicted on the monuments in human form is against such an opinion. The myth of Horus, the god of light, is conspicuously suggestive of incarnation, growth, and exaltation to the rulership of the world. Born of Osiris and Isis, filled with life and wisdom, victorious over the prince of darkness, ascending to the throne of his father, who still lives in the stars, and dwells in the phenix, and at the same time rules over the kingdom of departed souls, Horus would seem to exhibit a manifestation of Deity remarkably analogous to Jesus Christ. In the point of analogy named, even the Hindu Krishna scarcely shows a more notable ideal of God manifest in human forms of life and action. The hymns and prayers addressed to Ra and to Osiris are also filled with sentiments of the highest religious character, showing beyond question that, however mixed with mystic superstitions, the old

---

genii into beings, acting and feeling as human beings of decided character."—*Life in Ancient Egypt*, p. 263. Trans. by Tirard. London, 1894. Wiedemann (*Religion of the Ancient Egyptians*, London, 1897) maintains that "the idea of an animal incarnation of deity is thoroughly Egyptian" (p. 173), and was in accord with that ancient people's incapacity for abstract thought (p. 175). "In fixing upon certain animals as being respectively the incarnations of certain deities, the Egyptian was guided by what he considered the salient characteristics of the different divinities and of the different animals in question" (p. 178). "The death of the sacred animal did not involve the death of the god whom it represented, nor the loss of its own personal identity. Though the dislodged deity at once sought fresh incarnation in another animal of the same species and appearance as that which had died, the soul of the latter was immortal. As the dead man became an Osiris, so did the dead Apis become an Osiris Apis, the dead ram an Osiris ram, etc. In all these cases the same rites were performed for the animal as for the human mummy" (p. 182).

GREEK AND ROMAN IDEAS OF GOD. 31

Egyptian was possessed of some very exalted and worthy conceptions of God.

A glance at the religion of the Greeks shows among the first things to be noticed the human character of all its deities, and a familiar geneal- Greek ideas of ogy of the principal gods. Zeus, "the deity. father of gods and of men," is himself the offspring of Kronos and Rhea, who sprang from Ouranos and Gaia, and were thus conceived as offspring of heaven and earth. And all the myths and legends of the ancient Greeks move about this central notion of a remarkably humanlike intercourse between gods and men. Zeus is addressed in the Homeric poems as "Our Father,"[1] and the great artists of Greece, whenever they would set in painting or in sculpture the mightiest of all the gods, presented him in majestic human form.

The Latin mythology had much in common with that of the Greeks, but it was modified to accord with national characteristics of the Roman people. Janus was the mightiest Latin mythology. divinity who held the keys, and opened and shut the gates of heaven and earth. Jupiter, Juno, Vesta, Mars, Apollo, and the others figured as so many ideals of

---

[1] Thus in the *Odyssey*, i, 45 and 81, Athena addresses the son of Kronos in the words ὦ πάτερ ἡμέτερε—*O our Father*. Compare "Father Zeus" in *Od.*, v, 7; vii, 331; *Il.*, iii, 276, 320. A likeness may, perhaps, be traced between the myth of Athena springing in full panoply from the brain of Zeus, and the figure of Wisdom in Prov. viii, 22-31, "set up from everlasting, possessed by Jehovah from the beginning, daily his delight, rejoicing always before him."

heavenly power and excellence, and each one of them was assumed to be capable of more or less actual realization in human life. The deification of the Roman emperors was in its way a witness to the very human conceptions of deity which appear alike in the religions of Italy and Greece. So simple and familiar were the ideas of incarnation throughout the Roman empire in the time of Paul that when the people of Lystra saw the healing of a cripple by the word of the apostle they cried out, "The gods are come down to us in the likeness of men" (Acts xiv, 11).

It is not necessary, for our purpose, to examine the less historic religions for evidences of the idea of incarnation, or its virtual equivalent, in the concept of God as it has found varied expression among the tribes of men. But the widest induction and the most thoroughgoing analysis of the facts do not sustain the

Not evolved from human reasoning. hypothesis that the idea of God was ever evolved out of human reasonings.

The lowest savage tribes are not proven to be destitute of the idea of one Supreme Being. It is even surprising to find among some of the uncivilized races, "who live nearest to the open heart of nature," and have not been perverted by "vain reasonings," "foolish questions," and "endless genealogies," relatively pure and exalted concepts of one Supreme Being, as, for example, "the Great Spirit," commonly so called among the American Indians. Polytheism and fetichism and totemism are sometimes found in connection with the concept of one GOD-OVER-ALL, and we are of opinion

BIBLICAL ANTHROPOMORPHISM. 33

that, to a greater extent than has been generally imagined, we may trace in all the known religions of mankind evidences of one Supreme God and Father of all working to make himself known to his offspring, who, as Paul truly says, have quite generally "not approved of having (the) God in their knowledge" (Rom. i, 28), and so, though "knowing God, glorified him not as God, neither gave thanks; but became vain in their reasonings, and their senseless heart was darkened" (verse 21).

Now, it is a remarkable fact that the various concepts of God imaged forth in the mythology of the ancient nations find more or less expression in the Hebrew Scriptures. *Biblical anthropomorphism.*
The anthropomorphism which appears in some of the ancient Hebrew writers has been offensive to modern readers, and has been pronounced low and crass. Jehovah's formation of man (Gen. ii, 7), his walking in the garden in the cool of the day (iii, 8), his smelling the sweet savor of animal sacrifice (viii, 21), his coming down to see the city and tower (xi, 5), his feasting with Abraham (xviii) and wrestling with Jacob at Peniel (xxxii, 24), his appearance as an angel (xvi, 7; Exod. iii, 2), his presence in the pillar of cloud and of fire (Exod. xiii, 21), his coming down on the top of Sinai and talking with Moses there (xix, 20), his appearance to Joshua as Captain of the host (Josh. v, 14)—these and other like theophanies seem very human. But why should we assume that this naïve and childlike conception of Jehovah is unworthy of

our heavenly Father in his desire to approach the heart of the children created in his image? It is in perfect keeping with all the biblical declarations of his lovingkindness and tender mercies and wonderful works for the children of men. It accords with the gracious Providence that "loved Israel when a child" (Hos. xi, 1) and bore them as on eagles' wings out of the house of bondage (Exod. xix, 4; Deut. xxxii, 11). "In all their affliction he was afflicted, and the angel of his presence saved them; in his love and in his pity he redeemed them; and he bore them and carried them all the days of old" (Isa. lxiii, 9). Although the heaven of heavens cannot contain him, and he inhabiteth eternity, yet his peculiar delight is to "dwell with him that is of a contrite and humble spirit" (Isa. lvii, 15). The Levitical tabernacle was a symbol and object-lesson of Jehovah meeting and dwelling with Israel (Exod. xxv, 22; xxix, 43).

If some Hebrew writers speak at times of God as being in the heavens and man upon the earth (Eccles. v, 2), others recognize his presence in every part of the universe (Amos ix, 2; Psa. cxxxix, 7-12). He is the invisible Power behind all the forms and forces of the world of sense. He waters the mountains from his chambers, sends forth springs into the valleys, causes the grass to grow, and plants the cedars of Lebanon (Psa. civ). His voice thunders in the heavens, the clouds are his pavilion, the lightnings are his arrows, the stormy winds and tempests that move earth and sea are but

Immanence in the world.

the blasts of the breath of his nostrils, the foundations of the mountains quake at his presence (Psa. xviii). And it is the privilege and blessedness of every trusting soul of man to "dwell in the secret place of the Most High, and abide under the shadow of the Almighty" (Psa. xci, 1). No myths or legends of the world have given so vivid a concept of God's immanence in all the visible forms of nature as that which appears in the ancient Scriptures of the Hebrew people.

But our comparative research among the many religions of mankind, both those which now exist and those of past ages and peoples whose records yet remain, shows that the God of love has not left himself without witness among any of the nations, but has been graciously caring for them all. Some writers seem to think that the numerous analogies between religious cults, and such striking correspondencies as are found between the life of Jesus and the legends of Gautama, the myth of Horus, and the avatars of Vishnu, throw this whole world of thought and fact into a chaos of vain superstitions. They accordingly disparage all religions along with their traditions. But our studies beget a very different conviction. In the most erratic forms of worship, among the most haggard superstitions of abject races, one may discern a very earnest "feeling after God" (comp. Acts xvii, 27), and such religious feeling is begotten by the "drawing" of the heavenly Father (John vi, 44). The only way by which God himself, or any superior intelligence, can

Witnessed in all nations.

communicate with one inferior is through signs, or a language which the lower being comprehends. Both the means of communication and the ideas conveyed may be very imperfect, and yet be the best which conditions will admit. The Old Testament revelations of God come confessedly piecemeal, here a little and there a little, and in like manner have all the peoples received whatever light and truth they possess. And thus in varying degrees "the invisible things of God since the creation of the world are clearly seen, being perceived through the things that are made, even his everlasting power and divinity" (Rom. i, 20). We accordingly believe that our Father in the heavens has been continuously through the ages making his gracious manifestations of himself known to men. He made himself known to the Melchizedeks and Jethros of ancient time as truly as to Abraham and Moses. The Wisdom from above has cried aloud in the high places and along the pathways of the sons of men, and made its appeal much after the manner of the Hebrew prophet: "If I be a father, where is my honor? and if I be a master, where is my fear?" (Mal. i, 6.) And the men who have heard the heavenly voice have shown "the work of the law written in their hearts, their conscience bearing witness therewith, and their thoughts one with another accusing or else excusing them" (Rom. ii, 15). The love and gracious condescension of our heavenly Father have thus also been manifest in the avatars and sundry myths of the nations, but the senseless and darkened heart has not apprehended

CHRIST THE SUPREME MANIFESTATION. 37

the real lesson. God so loves the world that he is ever calling: "I am your Father, and ye are mine offspring. I am a God merciful and gracious, slow to anger and abundant in loving-kindness and truth, but in your disobedience and consciousness of guilt ye have thought me vengeful. I am light, but ye have loved darkness rather than light, and so have failed to learn of me. Turn ye from all your evil ways, and know the riches of my real affection."

But while our heavenly Father left not himself without witness among the nations, all other and previous revelations of himself have been eclipsed by the incarnation and mediation of Jesus Christ, "who was manifested in the flesh, justified in the spirit, seen of angels, preached among the nations, believed on in the world, received up in glory" (1 Tim. iii, 16). All the marvelous revelations of God given in the books of Moses, and in the prophets, and in the Psalms, are consummated and superseded "by reason of the glory that surpasseth" (2 Cor. iii, 10) them all in the manifestation of the Christ of God; much more completely has this manifestation consummated and eclipsed the inferior revelations of the whole Gentile world. "When the fullness of the time came, God sent forth his Son, born of a woman, born under the law, that he might redeem them that were under the law, that we might receive the adoption of sons" (Gal. iv, 4, 5). Such an incarnation of God must needs reveal himself and be revealed as "the way, and the truth, and the life."

CHAPTER III.

IDEAS OF MEDIATION SYMBOLIZED IN PRIESTLY SERVICE AND IN THE LEVITICAL RITUAL.

IT is quite natural for any worshiper of a supernatural Power to resort for assistance to some mediator between himself and the Deity. This fact has been to some extent apparent among the devotees of all the religions of the world. Among savage tribes we note the need and the reverence felt for the medicine man, Primitive priesthood and mediation. the soothsayer, or the priest, who is supposed to possess some superior influence with the powers invisible. In the biblical narratives of early patriarchal times the head of the household acted as priest and mediator. Melchizedek is mentioned in Gen. xiv, 18, as "king of Salem" and "priest of God Most High." Noah, Abraham, Isaac, Jacob, and Jethro, priest of Midian, are represented as building altars, offering sacrifices, and calling upon God, as if acting the part of a mediator and intercessor. Especially noteworthy is the account of Abraham standing as an intercessor before Jehovah, and pleading for the cities of the plain when their enormous wickedness had exposed them to the sentence of destruction from the righteous Judge of all the earth. The hero of the book of Job is depicted as an ancient patriarch and priest, offering up burnt offerings for the

PRIESTLY MEDIATORS.   39

sins of his sons and daughters (Job i, 5). Such mediation, intercession, and sacrifice, whatever forms they take on among different peoples, are an obvious provision for the sense of spiritual need which is deeply felt in the heart of man. For men are the offspring of God, and they come into conscious being possessed of a religious nature that instinctively feels and yearns after the living God. And the most ancient forms of priestly mediation between man and God evince an inborn yearning of the soul for peace and favor with the Author of its being.

Moses is represented as preeminently a mediator between Israel and God. The people were filled with a deep sense of awe, and they said unto Moses, "Speak thou with us, and we will hear; but let not God speak with us, lest we die. . . . And they stood afar off, and Moses drew near unto the thick darkness where God was" (Exod. xx, 19, 21). We also read that "Jehovah spoke unto Moses face to face, as a man speaketh unto his friend" (Exod. xxxiii, 11; comp. Num. xii, 8; Deut. xxxiv, 10). We find remarkable examples of Moses pleading before Jehovah in Exod. xxxii, 31, 32, and Num. xi, 11-15, and in the first-mentioned intercession he is spoken of as "going up unto Jehovah" to make atonement for the sins of the people. Similarly Samuel the prophet is besought to pray for the sinful people that they may not die (1 Sam. xii, 19-23). He offered burnt offerings to Jehovah, cried out aloud unto Jehovah, and was signally answered in behalf of Israel (vii, 9, 10). In all this he acted the part of a mediator and priest.

Moses was of the tribe of Levi (Exod. ii, 1), and according to the Levitical tradition he consecrated his brother Aaron to the priesthood, and the sons of Aaron were thereafter set apart by a perpetual statute to execute the office of priest in Israel. According to Exod. xiii, 2, 12, 15; xxii, 29, Jehovah claimed all the firstborn of Israel as his peculiar possession, but he substituted the tribe of Levi for the firstborn of all the people, and ordained that they alone should minister in holy things before him (Num. iii, 12, 41, 45; viii, 16-19). The trustworthiness of this Levitical tradition has been questioned, for subsequent to the times of Moses we read of such men as Gideon and Samuel and David and Solomon and Elijah offering sacrifices before Jehovah, apparently without any knowledge of such exclusive right of the descendants of Aaron. The great prophets from Samuel to Jeremiah show no such respect for priesthood, burnt offerings, and sacrifices as a knowledge of such a Mosaic appointment of Aaron's sons and the elaborate ritual of Levitical worship would naturally command. The probability is that this elaborate ritual of priesthood and offerings and multiplied ceremonies was of slow growth, and did not reach the completeness in which it now appears in the Priest Codex of the Pentateuch until the time of Ezra and the second temple. But the story of the wandering Levite in Judg. xvii, 7-13, the eagerness of Micah

THE LEVITICAL MEDIATION. 41

to secure his priestly services, his subsequent capture by the Danites to be the priest of their tribe, and the fact that he is called "the son of Gershom, the son of Moses," and that "his sons were priests to the tribe of the Danites until the day of the captivity of the land" (xviii, 30), show the priestly standing of the Levites in those unsettled times. Moreover, the ministration of Eli, the priest, in a temple of Jehovah at Shiloh, and a going up "from year to year to worship and to sacrifice unto Jehovah of hosts in Shiloh," as recorded in 1 Sam. i, 3-9, point to a very ancient seat of Levitical worship at that place, where, according to Judg. xxi, 19, an annual "feast of Jehovah" was observed. The priestly prerogatives of the whole tribe of Levi are also clearly witnessed in Deut. xviii, 1-8.

But our concern is not so much with the history of the Levitical priesthood as with its mediatorial significance. The officiating priest at the altar of sacrifice acted not for himself alone. *Significance of Levitical mediation.* He was mediator and representative of other worshipers before God. He was required to care for everything pertaining to the altar and the holy places (Num. xviii, 5, 7), to offer incense, light the lamps, attend to the showbread, and keep the fire continually burning on the altar of burnt offerings. The priests were also to be teachers of the law (Lev. x, 10, 11; Deut. xxxiii, 10). Their highest service, however, was to officiate in the offering of the various sacrifices described in the elaborate ritual of Lev. i-vii. In this they appear as the divinely ordained representatives of all Israel. The most solemn and significant service, developed in the later history of the Levitical priesthood, was that of the high priest on the day of atonement. Having washed his body and put on the hallowed garments, he proceeded to offer the burnt offering and the sin offering to make atonement for himself and for his house (Lev. xvi, 2-6). After this he took the censer full of burning coals, and burned incense so that the fragrant cloud arising therefrom covered the mercy seat above the ark; then he took the blood of the bullock which served as a sin offering for himself, and afterward the blood of the goat which served as the sin offering of the people, and, passing within the inner veil, sprinkled the blood of bullock and goat upon the mercy seat, and thus "made atonement for himself, and for his household, and for all the assembly of Israel" (Lev. xvi, 12-17). In all this symbolical service the high priest appears as a representative of all Israel, a sanctified and sympathetic mediator between a sinful people and a holy God, and the mediation which he effects is supposed to accord with the holiness of God on the one hand, and the needs and necessities of the people on the other.

The office and work of the Levitical priesthood cannot be fairly set forth without at least a brief notice of the various offerings which were required by the laws and regulations of the Priest Code.

Sacrificial offerings. These sacrificial offerings early acquired the threefold character of (1) self-surrender and self-dedication of the worshiper to God, (2) thanksgiv-

SACRIFICIAL OFFERINGS. 43

ing for his benefits and mercies, and (3) propitiation for sin. Cain and Abel are represented as bringing fruits of the ground and firstlings of the flock to present before Jehovah, and both fruits and firstlings are called a מִנְחָה, *offering,* or gift (Gen. iv, 3-5). The burnt offerings of Noah after the flood (Gen. viii, 20-22) were of the nature of thanksgiving and dedicatory worship. The ancient records of the patriarchs show a noticeable connection of their sacrifices and their prayers. We are not able to determine how far the idea of sacrificial blood in the earliest times was conceived as an expiatory offering for sin, but it is evident that in every case the sacrifice offered was a formal expression of self-surrender to God. The animal sacrifice, in its pouring out of the warm lifeblood of the victim, was suggestive of a vicarious offering up of life in accordance with what was believed to be the good pleasure of God, and the accompanying acts of festivity and thanksgiving were expressive of the worshiper's trust in God and of his delight in the conscious acceptance of all his benefits.

The elaborate ritual of the Priest Code carefully distinguishes between bloody and bloodless offerings. The cereal offerings ("meal offerings") consisted of corn in the ear, fine flour, and cakes baked or fried, and were accompanied with olive oil, frankincense, salt, and wine (Lev. ii). These were associated with libations, or drink offerings, of wine, and both together were a devout acknowledgment, as stated in 1 Chron. xxix, 11-14, that

Cereal offerings.

all things in the earth and heaven belong to Jehovah, and that all offerings which man can make to God are but a giving back to him some respectful portion of what he himself bestowed.[1]

The offerings which involved the shedding of blood, according to the ritual of Lev. i-vii, were of four kinds:

Blood offerings. burnt offerings (עלה), peace offerings (זבח שלמים), sin offerings (חטאת), and trespass offerings (אשם). The first two were in large part, like the meal offering, expressive of self-dedication and thanksgiving. The "whole burnt offering" symbolized the offering up to God of all that the worshiper represented, himself body and soul, his family and household, his property of every sort. All these were regarded as God's gracious gifts to him, and were to be held in readiness for any service of God to which they might be put. The peace offering was a public declaration of peaceful and friendly relationship between the worshiper and his God. The sacri-

---

[1] The awful practice of offering human sacrifices is probably best explained as a giving up to God the best, the dearest, the most sacred treasure possible. Abraham's willingness thus to offer up his only son for a burnt offering obtained for him Jehovah's great blessing (Gen. xxii, 16, 17). Jephthah offered his daughter and only child as the noblest possible sacrifice (Judg. xi, 31, 39). The king of Moab in the extremity of battle as a last resort offered his eldest son as a burnt offering (2 Kings iii, 27). But the prophets of Jehovah condemned this practice (Mic. vi, 7; 2 Kings xvi, 3; xxi, 6; xxiii, 10); it is denounced as an "abomination to Jehovah" in Deut. xii, 31, and explicitly forbidden in the Levitical code (Lev. xviii, 21). The practice, however, shows to what extremes religious zeal will go in efforts to obtain and hold favorable relations to God. The devotion thus evinced may be most admirable, but its method of display barbarous and abominable.

ficial feast which accompanied it was a joyful expression of fellowship with God, as if the happy participants were really eating and drinking in the presence of Jehovah.[1]

But the sin offering and the trespass offering were preeminently designed to make atonement for the sins of the people. They presuppose a separation between the worshiper and God, and also a deep sense of guilt which must have, in order to remission, the shedding of the lifeblood of the vicarious victim. The law of the trespass offering (אָשָׁם), according to Lev. v, 14-vi, 7, and Num. v, 5-8, contemplated individual offenses which call for restitution. If the trespass were a criminal appropriation of another's goods, the guilty man was required to restore in full, and also to add a fifth of its value as a fine. When the offense was an act of carnal impurity with a bondmaid the priestly law contemplated the deed as an infringement of the rights of property which demanded open satisfaction (Lev. xix, 20-22). Probably also some similar thought of compensation for lost service, or of fine for censurable defect, entered into the reasons for the trespass offering required in the case of the Nazarite (Num. vi, 12) and of the leper (Lev. xiv, 11-18). The trespass offerings accord-

Trespass offerings.

---

[1] Sacrifices on high places, like the one indicated in 1 Sam. ix, 12, 13, 23-25, were obviously of the nature of a public banquet at which the people and their God feasted and rejoiced together. 1 Sam. xx, 29, is evidence that families were wont to observe such sacrificial meals together. Comp. also xvi, 2-5, and Gen. xxxi, 54.

ingly contemplated individual offenses involving the consciousness of personal guilt.

But among all these offerings the most solemn and impressive appears to have been the חַטָּאת, *sin offering*, the detailed ritual of which is read in Lev. iv, 1-v, 13. A specific order of procedure and various sacrificial victims were ordained according to the rank and position of those for whom atonement was to be made. But whether the offender be the anointed priest, the whole congregation, the civil ruler, or one of the common people, in every case the atonement called for the shedding of blood. The only apparent exception is that of one so poor as not to be able to bring even "two turtledoves or two young pigeons" (v, 11-13). But the flour which in such case was allowed as a substitute, was not to be mixed with oil or frankincense, but to be burned upon the altar, and upon "the fire offerings of Jehovah" (אִשֵּׁי יְהֹוָה). Thus it was made to partake of the atoning efficacy of the animal sacrifices and reckoned as a real sin offering. The representative and propitiatory character of the sin offerings is seen in the fact that they were required not only for individual offenses, and sins of ignorance, but also for the whole people. They were offered on the great national feast days, on the occasion of consecrating the priests, and at the dedication of the tabernacle. They appear in most solemn significance in the ritual of the day of atonement (Lev. xvi). Everything connected with the ceremonies of that day

The sin offering.

Day of atonement.

DAY OF ATONEMENT. 47

was of the most awe-inspiring character, and the service was ordained not for specific and individual sins, but rather to "make atonement for the holy sanctuary and the tent of meeting, and the altar, and the priests, and all the people of the assembly." After all the other expiatory rites of an individual character, and aside from those of the other annual feasts and of the new moons (Num. xxviii, 11-15), the ritual of the day of atonement on the tenth day of the seventh month assumes that there is yet some defilement or deficiency which ought to be provided for in most impressive form. And so on that day the high priest must take the censer full of burning coals from the altar, and sweet incense and the blood of the sin offering, and go within the veil and let the cloud of incense cover the mercy seat, and sprinkle the blood upon the mercy seat seven times.

The ceremonial of confessing all the iniquities of Israel over the head of the goat that was "sent away for Azazel into the wilderness," which formed also a notable part of the ritual *The goat for Azazel.* of the day of atonement, deserves at least a passing notice. Whatever the origin of this part of the ceremonies, and whatever the real meaning of the word Azazel,[1] the formal confession of all their sins and putting them upon the head of the goat, which "bore upon

---

[1] Azazel appears in the book of Enoch as the name of the leader of the evil angels, thus connecting this section of the Priest Code with the later Jewish angelology, and forming one of the many indications that this whole ritual of the day of atonement is of postexilian origin.

him all their iniquities unto a solitary land," was a striking symbolical picture of the expulsion of sin and iniquity from the people of Israel. It was a public declaration that the sins of all the people were now sent away from them unto their own place, transferred to the abode of the evil spirits in the desert.[1] Thus both the people and their dwellings would be conceived as purged from the guilt and judgment of transgressions.

The classic passage in the Levitical law which defines the symbolical import of the expiatory offerings of blood is Lev. xvii, 11: "The life of the flesh is in the blood, and I have given (appointed) it to you upon the altar to make an atonement for your souls: for it is the blood that makes atonement by reason of the soul (life)." It is not the mere blood, as a material substance, that possesses the efficacy here ascribed to it, but the blood yet warm with the life of the victim. When the worshiper brought his offering and placed his hands upon its head he openly confessed thereby his guilt and obligation, and must have conceived that the animal offered was in some sense a vicarious sacrifice for himself; and when the lifeblood was "poured out before Jehovah" the symbolic rite was itself a public declaration that the life of the victim without blemish or spot was substituted in the mercy of God for the life of the

Symbolical significance of the blood.

---

[1] Compare the "passing through waterless places" (Matt. xii, 43), and the "casting into the outer darkness" (Matt. viii, 12), and "departing into the fire prepared for the devil and his angels" (Matt. xxv, 41), as a going forth to one's appropriate place.

CONSUMING THE FLESH. 49

transgressor. Whether the blood were poured out at the foot of the altar, or sprinkled on the horns of the altar, or at the golden altar of incense, or on the mercy seat within the veil, it was in every case regarded as a divinely appointed offering to make atonement for the souls of men.[1]

In connection with these ideas of atonement, symbolized in the shedding of sacrificial blood, the disposition of the flesh of the animal victims was not without suggestions of purification. The burning of the fat upon the altar, as an offering made by fire unto Jehovah (Lev. iv, 26, 31, 35), signified a free offering up to God of the better part of the worshiper, and the burning of the flesh of the sin offering without the camp in the clean place where the ashes of the altar were carried (Lev. iv, 12, 21) suggested a complete removal of the sins of the flesh. For a thorough taking away of sin requires more than the atoning efficacy of the blood of expiation: there must be also a blotting out of all iniquity; and this was symbolized by devoting the flesh of the sin offerings, as if defiled by its contact with sin, to the consuming fire. *The consuming of the flesh.*

The word כָּפֵר and its derivatives, which are usually translated by *atone* and *atonement*, deserve a passing notice in connection with the Levitical laws of expia-

---

[1] This was obviously the opinion, as we shall see farther on, of the author of the Epistle to the Hebrews, who elaborates the idea in his ninth chapter, and concludes that "according to the law, I may almost say, all things are cleansed with blood, and apart from the shedding of blood there is no remission" (ix, 22).

50   THE MEDIATION OF JESUS CHRIST.

tion. The primary meaning seems to be indicated by a
Meaning of atonement. usage which involves the idea of *covering over*, or *hiding*. Thus in Gen. xxxii, 20, Jacob thinks that he can *cover* the face of Esau with such a princely gift that his injured brother will not look upon the wrongs of the past.[1] Hence easily arose the meaning of covering over in the sense of appeasing, pacifying, propitiating, and in the sacrificial codes of the later priestly legislation the atonement offered was conceived as covering, concealing, and blotting out the sins of the guilty. The individuals thus covered or atoned for were regarded as delivered from exposure to the penal consequences of transgression. And this entire sacrificial arrangement appears in the biblical record not as an invention of men, nor as a service which recognized any merit in the person who brought the offering, but as a conspicuous con-
Condemnation of sin. demnation of sin. It is Jehovah that has graciously provided this substitute of animal life for the life of the sinner, and has appointed the offering of blood upon the altar to make atonement for the guilty soul. It should also be noted that the Hebrew word commonly translated *mercy seat* is כַּפֹּרֶת, the *cover,* or lid, of the ark of the covenant. The ark contained the two tables of the Decalogue, God's testimony against sin, and this *capporeth,* or cover, was to be sprinkled with blood on the day of

---

[1] The word כסות is used in the same way in Gen. xx, 16, where Abimelech gives a thousand pieces of silver for a *covering* of the eyes of all who were with Sarah that they might not see the offense to which she had been exposed.

SYMBOLISM OF SACRIFICE.   51

atonement (Lev. xvi, 11-17), and was thus made a significant symbol of "mercy covering wrath."[1]

Further details of priestly mediation and of sacrifices for sin, according to the Levitical ritual, need not detain us. But we shall find in other Scriptures, and in the New Testament teaching, frequent allusion to the offerings of blood as an atonement for sin. How far these outward symbols of expiation entered into the eternal purpose of God, and were typical of holy mysteries which became manifest in the mediation of Jesus Christ, is a question not to be lost sight of as we pursue our inquiries. The Old Testament ritual of mediation and of service contains sundry object-lessons which were of the nature of a preparatory discipline, looking to the mediatorial ministry of the Son of God. And the same may be said of other religious systems which have served to cultivate the sense of spiritual need and to turn the yearnings of the human heart toward God. For all these methods of feeling after the Infinite Helper may be conceived as so many expedients through which the heart of unspeakable LOVE worketh to draw all men unto himself. They also evince the necessity which the guilty but penitent soul feels for some saving efficiency higher than himself in order to deliverance from the power of sin. Efficient rescue from depths of self-despair must needs come through some manner of suffering and sacrifice.

Force of sacrificial allusions.

---

[1] For fuller showing of this symbolism, see my *Biblical Hermeneutics*, p. 272, and *Biblical Apocalyptics*, p. 83.

One unavoidable conclusion, which forces itself upon us when we study those customs of priesthood and sacrifice which go back to primitive times, is that they are all the expressions of religious conviction, and evince the need, felt everywhere and at all times, of some kind of mediation between man and God. In earliest times the head of the family acted as priest and offered the sacrifice, as appears in the examples of Noah and Jacob and Job. Whether the Deity recognized were conceived as a household God, or the God of the tribe to which the worshiper belonged, or to the one God over all, the worship in its essential elements would be the same. Hence we are to recognize the real depth and significance of the lowest forms of sacrificial worship, and to note that they all indicate desire and effort on the part of the worshipers to be on good terms with God. The offering seems in all cases to have been prompted by the query, "Wherewithal shall I come acceptably before my God?" The answer, of course, may take on various phases at different times and places. It may be in the form of fruits, libations of wine, whole burnt offerings, the blood of choice victims from flock and herd, and even a human sacrifice. The principle is the same in all. Along with such a variety of offerings would be associated divers conceptions of propitiation, atonement, expiation, and reconciliation, as also divers notions of priesthood. But in all ministrations of this kind the priest acts the part of a mediator between God and man. As it is

Priesthood and sacrifice express deep religious convictions.

TYPES OF MORE PERFECT SACRIFICE. 53

well stated in Heb. v, 1, he is "taken from among men and appointed for men in things pertaining to God, that he may offer both gifts and sacrifices for sins, and bear gently with the ignorant and erring." And so, probably, the best explanation of priesthood and sacrifice, the wide world over, is that God himself thus put it into the heart of man to do his best to be on favorable terms with the Author of his being. Thus has the Father sought to draw men; but their forms of approaching him were often matters of their own devising.

According to Heb. x, 1-4, all the Levitical offerings were insufficient to perfect the worshiper. The blood of animal sacrifices cannot take away sins. But those symbolical and typical ministrations of mediation were a "shadow of the good things to come." They serve to illustrate and in their measure reveal the greater and more perfect sacrifice of Christ, and the nature of his divine-human media- *Typical of Christ's perfect mediation.* tion. The earlier forms of worship, regarded as divine institutions, were graciously provided to assist man in his earnest feeling after God. The heavenly Father overlooked the misconceptions, the ignorance, and the errors; but in the fullness of time he brought in the clearer light to make known the mystery and the purpose of the ages.

It is, accordingly, a great error to condemn, as some do, all the sacrificial offerings of the old time as inhuman, heathenish, and *Erroneous notions of offering blood.* barbarous, arising out of superstitious fear of a vengeful Deity. No doubt demoralizing superstitions have too largely prevailed, but the degrading conceptions of placating an offended Deity spring from false views of God. The deities of the heathen world were often thought of as arbitrary, lustful, passionate beings, who deceived men by delusive dreams and subjected them to cruel plagues in order to gratify old feelings of revenge. Service offered to such a deity would naturally contemplate the removal of his wrath and spite. But we cannot regard such notions of God as having ethical content or value. The profound views of sin and guilt symbolized in the Levitical cult impart a nobler aspect to all offerings of blood. With the Hebrews atonement meant a divinely provided means of making God and man at one. The guilt-laden soul sought peace with the Holy One by means of the most sacred token of self-surrender he could bring. The real object was not to placate a revengeful Power, but to offer a reasonable, holy, and acceptable sacrifice before the Giver of all life, who had himself graciously instituted this means of reconciliation.

CHAPTER IV.

IDEAS OF MEDIATION IN THE PROPHETS AND THE PSALMS.

WE find in the writings of the Hebrew prophets and also in the psalms the portrayal of mediatorial intercession and of vicarious suffering which presents a higher conception of approach unto God than that of offering animal sacrifices. *A deeper spiritual view.* Isaiah proclaims Jehovah as having no delight in the oblations and burnt offerings of a people whose worship is only an outward heartless formality, while they fail to put away their evil doings (Isa. i, 10-17). Similarly Micah declares (vi, 6-8) that righteous action, loving affection, and walking humbly with God is a better means of approaching Jehovah than "thousands of rams, or ten thousands of rivers of oil." Vainly will one offer up his firstborn child for the sin of his soul. God looks rather for a deep struggle of the soul after purity and righteousness that results in spiritual transformation. And in like manner the psalmists extol the thought that Jehovah's delight is in the doing of his will rather than in ritual sacrifices and offerings (Psa. xl, 6-8). The most acceptable "sacrifices of God are a broken spirit: a broken and a contrite heart, O God, thou wilt not despise" (Psa. li, 17).

For these inner struggles of the contrite soul partake more of the nature of God's own yearnings to bring the fallen and erring ones into the experience of holy life and peace.

And so in the prophets and the psalms of Israel we read many a portraiture of vicarious struggles, illustrative of the depths of Jehovah's tender feeling. The book of Hosea is remarkable for its doctrine of condemning judgment mixed with divine compassion. Israel is depicted as a faithless wife who has notoriously played the harlot in departing from Jehovah. Her guilt is set forth in the darkest colors, and the certainty of penal retribution is forcibly declared. Having sown the wind, she shall reap the whirlwind. Having plowed wickedness, she must needs reap iniquity. And yet through all this prophecy there breathes a spirit of divine affection for the sinful nation. Jehovah would fain receive back his faithless wife, notwithstanding all her running after other lovers. He cries out as if in bitter anguish: "O Ephraim, how shall I give thee up? O Israel, how shall I deliver thee over (to judgment)? My heart is turned upon me; my compassions are kindled together. I will not execute the fierceness of mine anger, I will not return to destroy Ephraim; for I am God and not man, the Holy One in the midst of thee" (xi, 8, 9). In a similar way Isaiah arraigns the "sinful nation, a people laden with iniquity, who have forsaken Jehovah and despised the Holy One of Israel" (i, 4), and he an-

TEACHING OF THE PROPHETS. 57

nounces that because of their evil doings the judgments of fire and desolation have visited the land. But at the same time he pleads with them to put away the evil of their doings, and "though their sins be as scarlet, they shall be as white as snow; though they be red like crimson, they shall be as wool" (i, 18). Jeremiah recalls the piety of Israel's youth, the love of her espousal in the wilderness (ii, 2), but he cries out in astonishment over her backslidings, and her "playing the harlot with many lovers" (iii, 1). If one runs to and fro through the streets of Jerusalem he will seek in vain to find a man that doeth justly, that seeketh after truth (v, 1). And he speaks out the feeling of Jehovah himself when he cries: "Oh that my head were waters, and mine eyes a fountain of tears, that I might weep day and night for the slain of the daughter of my people! . . . For they proceed from evil to evil, and they know not me, saith Jehovah" (ix, 1, 3). The righteous judgment of God was signally executed on the sinful nation by Assyria, the rod of his anger (Isa. x, 5), and by the chastisements and woes of the Babylonian exile; but in all their woes the lovingkindness of Jehovah continued toward them, and he brought his people back from the lands of their exile as he had in the older time brought them up out of the Egyptian bondage. His loving purpose of redemption never failed. The most remarkable prophetic portraiture of vicarious suffering is found in Isa. lii, 13-liii, 12. It is an old question of exegesis whether the

Jeremiah.

58   THE MEDIATION OF JESUS CHRIST.

Servant of Jehovah in this passage is the same "Israel my servant, Jacob whom I have chosen, the seed of Abraham my friend," so frequently mentioned in preceding chapters (xli, 8, 9; xlii, 1; xliii, 10; xliv, 1, 2, 21; etc.), or some one individual of the nation, or the Messiah. Our use of the prophecy, however, need not wait for a final determination of that question; for the ideals of vicarious suffering presented in the language of the prophet are essentially the same in all these expositions, for the character described is that of "a man of sorrows," who leads Zion out of captivity, gives his soul as a trespass offering for sin, and makes intercession for the transgressors. Whatever, therefore, the possible explanations of the whole passage, the ideal set before us is that of an individual.

Isa. l, liii.

1. In the preceding context (lii, 1-12) the restoration of Zion and Jerusalem is portrayed in lively form. The captive daughter of Zion is called upon to shake herself from the dust and to go forth out of captivity, assured that her exodus from present oppression shall be more glorious than that from the Egyptian bondage. "For Jehovah hath comforted his people, he hath redeemed Jerusalem, hath made bare his holy arm in the eyes of all the nations, and all the ends of the earth have seen the salvation of our God." In departing from the present house of bondage they need not go out in such haste as in the ancient exodus, for Jehovah will go before and behind them like a pillar of cloud and of fire (verse 12). Thereupon the prophet intro-

FIFTY-THIRD OF ISAIAH. 59

duces his graphic picture of the servant who shall act wisely and become highly exalted.

2. In this graphic outline we cannot fail to observe such remarkable contrasts as acting wisely and being exalted very high, but having his form marred more than any man, and being despised and rejected of men. He grows up as a tender plant, and as a root from the dry ground, but somehow he brings healing to a sick and sorrowing world. He is led as a lamb to the slaughter, and yet he divides spoil with the mighty. He is terribly stricken on account of the sins of the people, but he sees the fruits of the travail of his soul and is satisfied. He is even made a curse for others, being wounded and bruised for their sins and bearing their iniquities, but by his knowledge he succeeds in making many righteous. It even pleases Jehovah to bruise him and put him to grief, but, as a result, "the pleasure of Jehovah shall prosper in his hand."

3. Among the many facts of his humiliation and suffering is the notable statement of verse 6 that "Jehovah hath mediated in him (הִפְגִּיעַ בּוֹ) the iniquity of us all." The word which we here translate *mediated*, and which is commonly rendered *laid on,* or *made to light on,* is used in the same causative form (Hiphil), but intransitively, in verse 12, where it means *maketh intercession*. It indicates in both places the mediatorial soul-passion and struggle of personal intercession, and what is remarkable is that in verse 6 Jehovah himself is the causative subject of the intercession, and in verse 12 the suffering servant of Jehovah, who

pours out his soul unto death and bears the sin of many, is the one who intercedes for the transgressors. So it is Jehovah who causes the iniquity of others to strike (פגע) and work an agony of travail in the soul of his servant, and the servant's mediatorial intercession avails for the transgressors.

4. The final triumph and exaltation of this servant of Jehovah are as wonderful as his subjection to suffering. He becomes highly exalted, attracts the attention of many nations and kings, his days are lengthened, a great posterity is promised him, he brings righteousness to multitudes, his soul is satisfied with the result of its travail, and he is conceived at last as a great conqueror who divides the spoil among his mighty heroes. Though numbered with the transgressors, he is a revelation of the arm of Jehovah's power.

5. Well might Christian interpreters have ever recognized in this prophetic picture of "a man of sorrows" a striking portraiture of Jesus Christ. For, whatever collective idea may here as in other parts of this book attach to the "servant of Jehovah," this description obviously contemplates a person who is distinguished from the whole house of Israel and who suffers for transgressions not his own. No less than seven times is it said in one form or another that he was smitten for the sake of others, and verse 9 declares that he himself was guilty of no violence or wrong. After the manner of the sin and trespass offerings of the Levitical ritual, his soul was made an offering for sin, poured out unto death, and he bare the sin of many.

In many of the psalms we find an abundance of passionate soul struggles voiced in the poetic language peculiar to the Hebrew psalter. The so-called "penitential psalms" (vi, xxii, xxxviii, li, cii, cxxx, cxliii) are like so many cries out of the depths of profound humiliation over the consciousness of sin, and confessions that rescue must come, if it comes at all, from a loving-kindness of God which is able to blot out transgressions. Other portions of the psalter are also remarkable for the keen insight they show into the guilt of human sinfulness and the need of redemption by means of a spiritual power from on high. We select Psa. xxii for more special examination, inasmuch as this is exceptionally remarkable for its agonizing self-expression. *Penitential psalms.* *Psa. xxii.* Some expositors believe it to be a composition of David, describing a terrible struggle of soul through which he himself passed. Others have ascribed it to Hezekiah, and some to Jeremiah the prophet. Others discern in the pleading sufferer of this psalm a personification of Israel in exile, and not a few insist that the language can be legitimately explained only of the sufferings of Christ and the glorious results secured thereby. Whatever view one takes of its authorship and immediate occasion, the various sentiments of this impassioned lyric, like those of Isa. liii, are to be studied for their profound suggestions touching the personal agony that may be felt in mediatorial intercession.

The exclamation at the beginning implies a terrible

sense of abandonment by God: "My God, my God, why hast thou forsaken me?" This feeling of rejection is the more amazing and impressive in view of the supplicant's continual cry, and the trust and deliverance of his fathers, as stated in verses 1-5. He thinks of himself as a writhing worm rather than as a man, an object of reproach and contempt among the people. All who gaze upon him in his agony treat him with derision; they laugh him to scorn, wag their heads, and cry out with biting sarcasm:

> "Roll it on Jehovah; let him deliver him;
> Let him rescue him, for he delighted in him."

In the midst of this great distress he finds no deliverer at hand, although God has been his trust from infancy. The following words show the extremity of his affliction:

> "Many bulls have compassed me about,
> Strong ones of Bashan have surrounded me.
> They have opened their mouth upon me,—
> As a lion tearing and roaring.
> Like waters am I poured out,
> And all my bones are sundered;
> My heart has become like wax,
> Melted in the midst of my bowels.
> My strength is dried up like a potsherd,
> And my tongue is cleaving to my jaws;
> And thou dost set me in the dust of death.
> For dogs have compassed me about;
> A crowd of evildoers have encircled me.
> They have pierced my hands and my feet,
> I can number all my bones;
> They keep looking and gazing at me.
> They divide my garments among them,
> And upon my vesture they cast lots."

TWENTY-SECOND PSALM. 63

In this extremity of woe he directs his prayer again to Jehovah (verses 19-21), and suddenly a marvelous answer comes. עֲנִיתָנִי, *Thou hast answered me,* he cries;

> "I will declare thy name to my brethren;
> In the midst of the assembly will I praise thee."

The remainder of the psalm (verses 23-31) is a triumphal declaration of the result of his sufferings and his prayers. He seems to struggle up out of depths of agony into heights of power, whence he calmly surveys "all the ends of the earth" returning to Jehovah and bowing down before him as their rightful ruler, whose righteousness is to be celebrated through all generations.

This remarkable poem abounds with metaphors which run into hyperbole, but the extravagance of the figures serves to intensify to the uttermost the portraiture of personal affliction. The psalm is usually reckoned among the Messianic psalms, but it contains expressions which are inapplicable to Jesus Christ. This much, however, should be said, that the sufferer who gives utterance to these impassioned words is an innocent sufferer, and in all his agony he gives forth no vent of anger against those who revile him. No other Old Testament scripture suggests in equal space so many facts mentioned in connection with the crucifixion of the Son of man. Verse 1 was uttered by him on the cross (Matt. xxvii, 46; Mark xv, 34). The wagging of heads, the mockery and sarcasm, the thirst, the piercing of hands and feet, the parting of his raiment and casting lots for it, are all mentioned in the Gospels in describing the last agony of Jesus. And the last word of the psalm, עָשָׂה, *he has done* it, or *it is accomplished,* reminds us of Jesus's last word, according to John xix, 30, τετέλεσται, *it is finished.* All these facts along with the representative character of the sufferer, who assumes that his triumph through unspeakable agony is destined to secure the redemption and reunion of "all the families of the nations," makes the twenty-second psalm a typical prophetic oracle. It sets before us an ideal Israelite, in whom is no guile, subjected to a passion of soul that makes him a representative partaker of the sufferings of Christ and of the glories destined to follow. For the speaker in this psalm is a remarkable type of mediatorial suffering. His own personal experience of woe and deliverance enabled him to voice an ideal which has found its most complete fulfillment in the Christ of the New Testament.

A study of the foregoing ideas of priestly and sacrificial mediation, as found in the Hebrew scriptures, will enable us also to see how this general concept of mediatorial intercession and salvation became naturally associated with Israel's Messianic hope. The Lord who sits at the right hand of Jehovah, according to Psa. cx, and is destined to subdue and judge among the nations, is declared by the oath of Jehovah to be "a priest forever after the order of Melchizedek." The Epistle to the Hebrews (chaps. vi and vii) magnifies

Connection with Israel's Messianic hope.

this saying as a most significant ideal of the priesthood of Jesus Christ, who is proclaimed (viii, 1, 2) as "a high priest who sat down on the right hand of the throne of the Majesty in the heavens, a minister of the sanctuary, and of the true tabernacle, which the Lord pitched, not man." The significance of this conception of Melchizedek will be considered farther on.

The language of Dan. ix, 24, is worthy of attention as indicating the writer's idea of the termination of an old order, the end of certain forms of transgression and sin, and the introduction of a new order of everlasting righteousness. The passage is best translated in the form of Hebrew parallelisms:

Dan. ix, 24.

"Seventy heptades are decreed upon thy people and upon thy holy city,
To close up the transgression and to consummate sins,
And to expiate iniquity and to introduce eternal righteousness,
And to seal up vision and prophet, and to anoint a holy of holies."

The expiation of iniquity here spoken of seems to be some propitiatory mediation of epochal significance, which is to be effected at the point of time to which the prophecy refers. The sealing up of vision and prophecy most naturally means the fulfilling and cessation of prophetic oracles by the opening of the Messianic age of universal knowledge (comp. Isa. xi, 9). The consecration of a new holy of holies implies the institution of a "greater and more perfect tabernacle," with its new and living way of entrance for all the pure in heart (comp. Heb. ix, 11; x, 19). It is easy to see how these references to some new and superior methods of expiation were capable of a special Messianic application, and the song of Zacharias contains (Luke i, 68, 77) profound conceptions of "redemption for his people," "knowledge of salvation," and "remission of sins," which formed a part of Israel's Messianic hope as held among the most pious of the nation. And it was thus through sacrifices, and symbolic forms of worship, and soul-stirring oracles of prophets, and prayers of the psalmists, that God's purpose and the mystery of the ages were slowly working in the course of Israel's history and preparing the way for a clearer revelation.

THE SAYINGS OF JESUS. 67

CHAPTER V.

DOCTRINE OF JESUS IN THE SYNOPTIC GOSPELS.

THE beginning of the Epistle to the Hebrews assumes the variety and the progressive character of divine revelation: "God, having of old time spoken unto the fathers in the prophets by divers portions and in divers manners, hath at the end of these days spoken unto us in (the person of one who has the position and quality of a)[1] Son, whom he appointed heir of all things, through whom also he made the ages." It is important for us above all things in this study of mediation to learn as accurately as possible the teachings of Jesus Christ himself, and it is the prevalent belief that the Synoptic Gospels, Matthew, Mark, and Luke, furnish us with the most exact tradition of the words of our Lord.

<small>Relative importance of Jesus's words.</small>

Of all the reported sayings of Jesus, bearing on the doctrine of mediation, the most noteworthy is probably that which is recorded in Matt. xx, 28, and Mark x, 45: "The Son of man came not to be ministered unto, but to minister, and to give his life a ransom for

---

[1] All that is expressed in this parenthesis is implied by the absence from the Greek text of the article in the phrase ἐν υἱῷ; not ἐν τῷ υἱῷ, nor ἐν τῷ υἱῷ αὐτοῦ.

68   THE MEDIATION OF JESUS CHRIST.

many." The main question in this passage touches the precise meaning of the last three words, *a ransom for many* (λύτρον ἀντὶ πολλῶν). In defining the word λύτρον, *ransom*, in such a statement as is here made, we cannot fairly ignore the usage and connotation it holds in the Septuagint version of the Old Testament.[1] In Exod. xxi, 30, it means the price that may lawfully be put upon the life of one who is exposed to the penalty of death, and by the payment of which he is to be released from such penal exposure. In Exod. xxx, 12, the word is employed to designate the poll tax of half a shekel which "every man shall give as a ransom for his soul unto Jehovah." In Lev. xxv, 51, it stands for the price paid for the liberation of one who has been sold into bondage. The word is also used in connection with the redemption of land that had been sold (Lev. xxv, 24), and the redemption of the produce of the land which by the law of tithing belonged unto Jehovah (Lev. xxvii, 31). In all these examples and illustrations of the ransom the main idea is that of substituting one thing for another. Hence the preposition ἀντί, *for, in place of,* is naturally employed in Matt. xx, 28, as most consonant with the idea of a *ransom price*.[2] The Son

"Ransom for many."

---

[1] It is used alike for the translation of פִּדְיוֹן, כֹּפֶר, and גְּאֻלָּה, all of which have in common the meaning of *ransom, redemption,* or *price of redemption*. The word ἀντίλυτρον in 1 Tim. ii, 6, seems to be substantially identical in meaning, and λύτρωσις (Luke i, 68; ii, 38; Heb. ix, 12) and ἀπολύτρωσις (Rom. iii, 24; Eph. i, 7, 14; Col. i, 14; Heb. ix, 15) also have the same general significance and connotation.

[2] The preposition περί is, however, used in connection with λύτρα in the Septuagint of Num. xxxv, 31.

of man gives his life as a ransom price for the liberation of many who are assumed to be held under some sort of bonds. In what this bondage consists nothing in the text or context tells; but the statement in Matt. xxvi, 28, that his blood "is shed for many unto remission of sins," and the use of the verb λυτρόω in Titus ii, 14, and 1 Pet. i, 18, in the sense of "ransoming from all iniquity," and "ransoming from a vain manner of life," are good evidence that the ransom contemplated by Jesus in the text under discussion is deliverance from the bondage of sin. The figure of "selling one's self to do evil" would probably have been familiar to readers of the Old Testament (comp. 1 Kings xxi, 20, 25; 2 Kings xvii, 17), and Paul develops the idea at length (Rom. vi, 16-23; vii, 14, 23). What Jesus himself taught about the impossibility of serving two masters and about repentance and remission of sins accords with the same idea. When, therefore, he declares that he "came to give his life a ransom for many" the most natural and obvious thought suggested is that of redemption from the bondage of sin. But the *process* or *mode* by which this redemption is accomplished is not here described; nor need we assume that the "giving of his life" in this text refers exclusively to his death on the cross. Jesus foretold his death and spoke of its necessity (comp. Luke ix, 22; xxiv, 7, 26, 46; John xii, 23-27); he recognized the closing period of his earthly life as a crucial hour; but when he says, "For this cause came I unto this hour," we are not justified in the inference that the events of his death on the cross were of more value in his work of mediation than many other events of his life. We must duly recognize all the great facts of his incarnation, and his resurrection and ascension, and the apostolic teaching that he ever lives to make intercession for us. The sacrifice of his life includes also every cup of agony which he drank (comp. Matt. xx, 22; xxvi, 42; John xviii, 11), and the baptism of overwhelming trials which he underwent (comp. Mark x, 38; Luke xii, 50). His severe temptations in the wilderness, his longsuffering with a "faithless and perverse generation" (Matt. xvii, 17), his upbraiding of Chorazin and Bethsaida, his weeping over Jerusalem, and his amazement and bloody sweat in Gethsemane were all of them together only a part of the mediatorial struggle involved in his giving his life a ransom for many. He recognized it as the high purpose of his mission "to seek and to save that which was lost" (Luke xix, 10). He "came not to call the righteous, but sinners" (Matt. ix, 13), and he would search far and labor long to gather in "the lost sheep of the house of Israel." In all these statements we read the struggle of an intensely sympathetic friend of the sinner, and, like the ideally good shepherd, ready to lay down his life for the sheep. He endured all manner of opposition of sinners, and "resisted unto blood, striving against sin" (Heb. xii, 3, 4).

His entire life a ransom.

Such a giving of his life for the ransom of many from the bondage of sin need not and ought not to be

CHRIST AS A RANSOM. 71

complicated in thought by attempts to discover in the mediation of Christ something analogous to every idea which the figure of a ransom suggests. Ignore remote analogies. In what manner this heavenly Redeemer accomplishes his ministry of redemption is a legitimate inquiry, and will be considered in the pages which follow; but when Jesus says that his life was given to bring about the liberation of mankind from the power of sin, it diverts attention from his main thought when one asks "to whom the ransom was paid," and how it could be an "equivalent satisfaction" of the debt which guilty man owed God.[1] Confusion of thought must needs attend the effort to press into dogmatic significance every suggestion and implication of a metaphor. In such a text as Deut. vii, 8—"Jehovah *redeemed* you out of the house of bondage, from the hand of Pharaoh king of Egypt"—we

---

[1] It seems hardly necessary to make mention of the old patristic fiction of God giving the soul of Jesus as a ransom to Satan, who was thought of as holding humanity in captivity. Such an importance accorded to Satan formed part of a fanciful and absurd demonology now quite effectually exploded. The later Anselmic theory of substituting the infinite merit of Christ's sufferings as an equivalent satisfaction for the infinite demerit of sin moves in a realm of thought quite foreign to the Scriptures. It has a logical affinity with the later Romish doctrine of indulgences, and with ultra Antinomianism and its fictions of the imputation of man's guilt to Christ, and of Christ's personal righteousness to the elect. The originators and advocates of these theories failed to perceive that a ransom of such infinite merit, and such a complete satisfaction of justice, logically leave no reasonable ground for the doctrine of salvation by grace. Whatever grace may be alleged in such a monergistic scheme is by the hypothesis so essentially compulsory as to rob it of all the real qualities of mercy. But perhaps the worst feature of this monergistic scheme was its sovereign exclusion of the nonelect from any share in the imputed righteousness of Christ,

do not suppose that a ransom price was paid to Pharaoh or to the Egyptians; nor do we even imagine that Sheol and death receive a stipulation when we read Hos. xiii, 14: "From the hand of Sheol I will ransom them; from death I will redeem them." The great fact in this case is that Jesus Christ entered into all the experiences of human life. He was tempted in all points as we are; he confronted the scorn and malice and violence of a hostile world; and in all this struggle he sacrificed himself and gave up his own life to rescue men from sin. It seems, therefore, irrelevant and idle to inquire after some particular creditor to whom such a ransom must have been paid. When we think properly of a deliverer who of his own good will subjects himself to a fearful struggle, involving the sacrifice of his life to rescue others from the peril of death, we do not ask *to whom,* but rather *for whom,* that costly price of self-sacrifice was paid. Such ransoms are prompted by the purest emotion of love, one noble life is given instead of the many exposed to death, and the sufferings involved are even gladly borne for the sake of the rescued ones and the glory that must result from such a work of redemption.

Another important saying of our Lord bearing on the doctrine of his mediation is found in connection with the last supper, when he took the cup and gave it to the disciples, and said, according to Matt. xxvi, 28, "Drink of it all ye; for this is my blood of the covenant, which is shed for many (περὶ πολλῶν) unto remission of sins." The

<small>Words of Jesus at last supper.</small>

BODY AND BLOOD. 73

parallel text in Mark xiv, 24, reads, "This is my blood of the covenant, which is shed for many" (ὑπὲρ πολλῶν). The reading in Luke xxii, 20, is peculiar, is omitted from some ancient manuscripts, and has been thought by some critics to be an interpolation:[1] "This cup is the new covenant in my blood, that which is poured out for you" (ὑπὲρ ὑμῶν). Paul's statement in 1 Cor. xi, 25, corresponds closely to that of Luke: "This cup is the new covenant in my blood: this do, as oft as ye drink, in remembrance of me." These solemn words, together with what Jesus said in the same connection about eating the bread as a symbol of his body given and broken for them, have obvious allusion to some typical significance in the passover meal which our Lord and his disciples were eating together. They clearly imply that in some sense he became for them a true paschal lamb and all else which the paschal supper signified; and it accords with this idea that, according to Luke xxii, 16, 18, he himself partook of it neither by eating nor drinking. All the Synoptists record Jesus's refusal to drink thenceforth from the fruit of the vine until he should drink it new (καινόν) in the kingdom of God. But if we suppose that he ate of the paschal lamb with them, but declined to eat of the bread and drink of the cup, we obtain nothing of essen-

---

[1] Thus Westcott and Hort, after stating the difficulties of the critical problem, observe: "These difficulties, added to the suspicious coincidences with 1 Cor. xi, 24, 25, and the transcriptional evidence given above, leave no moral doubt that the words in question were absent from the original text of Luke, notwithstanding the purely western ancestry of the documents which omit them."—*Notes on Select Readings*, p. 64.

tial value for determining the significance of our Lord's words on the occasion. He declared the bread to be his body and the cup his blood of the covenant which was shed for many, and the language can mean no less than that he himself was in some sense given as a sacrifice for many, whether he himself at that time ate of the paschal lamb or not. It is also well to note in passing that Paul conceived Christ as "our passover slain" (1 Cor. v, 7). Whatever the particular forms observed in the course of the paschal meal in the time of our Lord, there can be no doubt that the feast itself was celebrated as a memorial of Israel's deliverance from the bondage of Egypt (comp. Exod. xii, 14; xiii, 9). The story of that deliverance could not well be told apart from the memorable sprinkling of the blood of the first paschal lamb upon the side posts and lintel of the houses to defend the dwellers therein against the destructive plague. Thus the entire feast of the passover was on the one hand essentially a memorial of Israel's redemption unto Jehovah; on the other hand, the words "my blood of the covenant," used by Jesus according to all the Synoptists, can hardly be explained otherwise than as a conscious appropriation of the language of Exod. xxiv, 8, where the reference is to the blood of burnt offerings and peace offerings sacrificed unto Jehovah; but the emphatic statement that he would not drink of this symbol of the blood of the covenant until he should drink it καινόν, *new in kind,* with them in the heavenly kingdom, reminds us of the words of Jeremiah (xxxi, 31-34)

BLOOD OF A NEW COVENANT. 75

about the new covenant between Israel and Jehovah,[1] and helps to point out the spiritual significance of all this language of Jesus at the paschal meal. It was a new kind of eating and drinking to which he would elevate their thoughts by means of this symbolic meal, a feasting together in the heavenly kingdom of his Father.[2] The eating of his body and drinking of his blood must mean a partaking of his spirit and of the eternal life which he imparts (comp. John vi, 53-58, 63). He surrenders himself, body and soul, to the death of the cross, for the redemption of many from a worse than Egyptian bondage. For it is only as his spotless life is thus freely offered that he himself becomes the potent means and mediator of human salvation. The shedding of the blood of this paschal lamb has for its object, as Matthew (xxvi, 28) records it, "remission of sins." We cannot therefore with proper regard to the simplest suggestions of the language and its occasion divorce from the words of Jesus at the last supper the then current ideas of atonement through the sprinkling of blood. One may appropriately say, in the language of Isa. liii, 10, "It pleased Jehovah to bruise him and to make his soul an offering for sin." The institution of the new covenant of his gospel, like

---

[1] The use made of this passage from Jeremiah in Heb. viii, 6ff., is worthy of careful study in connection with the words of Jesus. The plan of our treatise requires us to treat it in another connection.

[2] One might compare the figure of "reclining with Abraham and Isaac and Jacob in the kingdom of heaven" (Matt. viii, 11), and the blessedness of those "who are bidden to the marriage supper of the Lamb" (Rev, xix, 9).

that of the old covenant of Mount Sinai, was accordingly ratified by the shedding of blood, and it was the blood of Jesus, the blood of the new covenant, shed for many because given for the life of the world.

It appears from the foregoing discussion that the teaching of Jesus touching his own mediation, as found in the Synoptic Gospels, is not extensive, but what we do find is very direct, positive, and unmistakable. And we cannot fairly or satisfactorily explain his language without admitting the obvious allusions to Old Testament ideas of atonement and redemption.

CHAPTER VI.

DOCTRINE OF JESUS IN THE FOURTH GOSPEL.

THE peculiarities of the Fourth Gospel are such that it has become common in biblical theology to treat its contents of doctrine as having received some measure of coloring from the *Peculiarities of John's gospel.* subjective and mystic type of thought which belonged to the mind of the writer. The critical questions of its date and authorship have undergone the most searching investigation, and resultant opinions are divided; but it is now generally conceded that this unique and matchless portraiture of Christ was abroad upon its world-wide mission in the early part of the second century. For myself, I do not find any hypothesis of its origin is so well supported as the common tradition of the early Church, and my own reading and meditation on the subject during the past forty years have steadily deepened my conviction that this remarkable Gospel is a genuine composition of the apostle John. It is not difficult to believe that after surviving his Lord nearly two generations, and repeating over and over the divine thoughts which he had learned from him, those thoughts would take on a cast and style peculiar to the aged disciple and apostle.

But so far as this Gospel presents the doctrine of mediation and atonement for sin it confirms and supplements the teaching of the Synoptics. In John i, 29, 36,

Confirms and supplements Synoptics. Jesus is pointed out by John the Baptist as "the Lamb of God, who takes away the sin of the world." This language contemplates a sacrificial lamb, for it is one that removes or *bears away* (αἴρων) sin, a statement which at once suggests to anyone familiar with the Jewish Scriptures the idea of propitiatory offerings.[1] This Lamb of God is one who makes atonement for "the sin of the world;" and while the statement is represented as coming from John and not from Jesus, it nevertheless accords with what appears to be the teaching of Jesus in this Gospel. For this idea of a world-atonement through the offering up of a most precious sacrifice is the essential doctrine of John iii, 14-16: "As Moses lifted up the

John iii, 14-16. serpent in the wilderness, even so must the Son of man be lifted up: that whosoever believeth in him may have eternal life. For God so loved the world, that he gave his only begotten Son, that whosoever believeth on him should not perish, but have eternal life." It is an old question of exegesis whether all these are words of Jesus or an enlargement of his words made by the evangelist. The

---

[1] So Meyer: "Christ was, as the Baptist here prophetically recognizes him, the antitype of the Old Testament sacrifices: he must, therefore, as such, be represented in the form of some animal appointed for sacrifice; and the appropriate figure was given not so much in the law as by the prophet (Isa. liii, 7, 10), who, contemplating him in his gentleness and meekness, represents him as a sacrificial lamb, and from this was derived the form which came to be the normal one in the Christian manner of view."—*Critical and Exegetical Handbook, in loco.*

only trustworthy answer seems to be the general one that the teaching of Jesus had so thoroughly taken possession of the evangelist's thought and life as to find its true expression not in the exact terms employed by the Lord, but rather in the language and style of the disciple. Whether Jesus uttered these sentiments near the beginning or at the end of his ministry is a question of no essential importance to John. His aim is to present Jesus for all that he is worth to the believer (comp. xx, 31), and the words to Nicodemus in iii, 14-16, fairly interpreted, include the following truths: (1) The mediatorial offering of Christ has its origin in the love of God, which is a world-embracing love. (2) The offering involves the most affecting of all possible sacrifices, the giving of an only begotten Son[1] for the rescue and the eternal life of the perishing world of mankind. (3) The Son thus offered is in some sense a vicarious sacrifice for those who are liable to perish, but who, through faith in him, may have eternal life and be saved. (4) In the course of this divine procedure the Son of man is exalted before the eyes of men (comp. the προεγράφη, *openly portrayed*, of Gal. iii, 1) "even as Moses lifted up the serpent in the wilderness" (comp. Num. xxi, 9). (5) In order to accomplish this salvation of the world it was somehow necessary (δεῖ) that the Son of man should be thus lifted up (ὑψωθῆναι). This *being lifted up* refers most

---

[1] The offering of "the only begotten Son" may find some measure of its impressiveness in a conscious allusion to the offering of Isaac by Abraham in Gen. xxii, 2, 16.

80   THE MEDIATION OF JESUS CHRIST.

naturally to his being lifted up on the cross,[1] and the voluntary surrender of himself to the death of the cross is the mode, according to John's Gospel, in which the love of God asserted itself and became effectual for the salvation of the world.

This giving of the Son of man for the life of the world is further set forth in the remarkable words of John vi, 50, 51, and what is written in connection with them. The figure here is not that of a sacrificial victim offered on the cross, but of living bread out of heaven: "I am the living bread which came down out of heaven: if any man eat of this bread, he shall live forever: yea, and the bread which I will give is my flesh, for the life of the world." But the provision of such heavenly food necessarily involves the sacrifice of the life of the Son of man; for he goes on to say that, "except ye eat the flesh of the Son of man and drink his blood, ye have not life in yourselves. He that eateth my flesh and drinketh my blood hath eternal life; and I will raise him up at the last day." This is no doubt mystical language and is to be spiritually interpreted (comp. verse 63), but it has the most vital relation to the doctrine involved in the words of the last supper touching the eating of his body and the drinking of his

Giving of his flesh and blood for the life of the world.

---

[1] Compare John viii, 28; xii, 32-34. In the last-named passage the writer understands Jesus to "signify by what manner of death he should die;" but the words "if I be lifted up from the earth" (ἐκ τῆς γῆς, *out of the earth*) are hardly compatible with the mere idea of being lifted up on the cross, and verse 33 has been suspected as an interpolation. But viii, 28, "When YE have lifted up the Son of man," indicates the crucifixion.

blood. The gracious provision of God in giving his Son that the world through him might be saved becomes effectual in the individual believer only as he personally accepts the wonderful gift of the Father's love, and inwardly appropriates the living bread from heaven. So "he that believeth hath eternal life" (verse 47).

The vicarious offering of his own life for the sake of others is also seen in John x, 11, 15, where Jesus declares himself the good shepherd who lays down his life for the sheep. *Dying for others.* The idea suggested in this illustration is not that of an expiatory offering for sin, but rather of an exposure to loss of life consequent upon faithful care of the flock. A similar thought is conveyed in the language of xv, 13: "Greater love hath no man than this, that a man lay down his life for his friends." A man may thus lay down his own life for the sake of his friends in one or another out of many ways; and yet it is in keeping with the imagery of offering the blood of life upon the altar to speak of all such modes of giving up one's life for the sake of another as examples of vicarious sacrifice without which there could have been no salvation of the one that was rescued. This idea certainly pervades the Gospel of John, and appears in the construction which the author puts upon the saying of Caiaphas, "that it was expedient that one man should die for the people, and that the whole nation perish not;" for he looked upon this utterance of the high priest as an inspired oracle, "that Jesus should die for the nation; and not for the nation only, but that he might also gather together into one the children of God that are scattered abroad" (xi, 50-52). The idea of sacrifice, even unto the laying down of life, appears also in the proverbial saying of xii, 24: "Except a grain of wheat fall into the earth and die, it abideth alone; but if it die, it beareth much fruit." This principle of sacrifice in order to reach some greater good is fundamental in the moral world, and the death of Jesus is its highest possible illustration.

But in no portion of the Fourth Gospel do we find a more impressive self-revelation of Jesus Christ as Mediator between God and man than in his high-priestly prayer in chapter xvii. With a sublime self-consciousness of oneness with the Father, and at the same time of oneness with the men who are given him out of the world, he stands as a great high priest who has already virtually passed into the heavenly places and "appears before the face of God for us" (comp. Heb. ix, 24). He is conscious of having come forth from the Father, of having glorified him on the earth, of having accomplished the ministry of his incarnation, and of having arrived at the crucial hour of leaving the world and being glorified with the glory which he had with the Father before the world was. He has manifested the Father's name and given his word to the disciples; and now, as he is about to leave them and go unto the Father, he prays for them that they may be kept and guarded from the evil of the world, and sanctified in the truth.

Intercessory prayer in chapter xvii.

THE MEDIATORIAL PRAYER. 83

As he had sanctified or consecrated himself in willing sacrifice, he prays that they also may be consecrated in a freewill offering of themselves in the truth. And finally he prays that they and those who should thereafter believe on him through their word "may all be one; even as thou, Father, art in me and I in thee, that they may be perfected into one; that the world may know that thou didst send me, and lovest them, even as thou lovest me." And so the one great Mediator pleads, desiring that those who are thus united in holy fellowship "be with me where I am, that they may behold my glory, which thou hast given me: for thou lovedst me before the foundation of the world."

This remarkable intercession is equivalent to a declaration on the part of Jesus that he came forth from God as a divinely appointed Revealer of the Father's grace and glory, and as a Mediator divinely consecrated to effect the perfect union and fellowship of God and all them that are sanctified in the truth. He alone can say to the Father, "They are thine: and all things that are mine are thine, and thine are mine: and I am glorified in them." After the manner of Heb. ii, 13, and its context, we may here behold the sanctifier and the sanctified "all of one," and we see the author of their salvation, made perfect through suffering, leading many sons into glory, and saying, "Behold, I and the children whom God hath given me."

The Gospel of John, then, so far as it reports any teaching of Jesus on the subject of his redemptive mediation and the offering of his own life for men, is in fundamental harmony with the Synoptists. The author understood these sayings of Jesus as conveying the most profound spiritual significance of sacrificial offerings. The life of Jesus was given in exhibition of God's boundless love to rescue a perishing world, and to provide eternal life to everyone who would personally appropriate the gift.

It is to be observed, however, that the Gospel records are not the class of biblical writings in which one should look to find any formal or extensive treatment of the doctrinal significance of Jesus's death. They are rather the memoirs of his words and works. They recount the facts of his birth, life, death, and resurrection, but they enter into no discussion of the doctrines of religion which are connected with those facts. It does not appear that Jesus himself furnished his disciples with detailed instruction on the significance of his laying down his own life for the world. His followers were strangely slow to understand what he did say to them on those matters (Mark ix, 32; Luke ix, 45; xviii, 31-44), but afterward they received a deeper insight, and recalled his words, and found them filled with a meaning which they had not comprehended while he was with them in the flesh (comp. John xii, 16; xiii, 7; xvi, 13). We may therefore expect to find in other New Testament writings a fuller statement of the mediatorial office and ministry of Jesus Christ.

Gospels not the place to look for doctrinal significance of Jesus's death.

CHAPTER VII.

DOCTRINE OF THE OTHER JOHANNINE WRITINGS.

THE doctrine of the First Epistle of John accords so closely with that of the Fourth Gospel that in now passing to a study of the apostolical epistles we may appropriately begin with this important document of the early Church. For though this epistle may be among the very latest products of the apostolic age its doctrine of the mediatorial work of Christ appears to be in substance identical with what we find in the very earliest examples of apostolic teaching. A remarkably close parallel to the great text in John iii, 16, is the comprehensive statement of 1 John iv, 9, 10, where, in immediate connection with the words "God is love," we read: "Herein was the love of God manifested in us, that God hath sent his only begotten Son into the world, that we might live through him. Herein is love, not that we loved God, but that he loved us, and sent his Son to be a propitiation for our sins." Verse 14 says that "the Father has sent the Son as Saviour of the world." Nothing is clearer in these statements than that the "propitiation for our sins" originates in the love of God. The work of Christ as "Saviour of the world" is not to appease a wrathful Deity, as was supposed in propitiatory sacrifices among the heathen,

Doctrine of the First Epistle.

but rather a move on God's part to provide a covering of sins. This word ἱλασμός, translated *propitiation*, is employed in the Septuagint for the Hebrew כִּפֻּרִים, *coverings*, in the sense of atonement for sin and the consequent pardon and removal of the sin. So in this epistle of John the manifestation of Christ was for the purpose of *taking away sin* (iii, 5; comp. John i, 29), and thus *destroying the works of the devil* (iii, 8). This provision for the uttermost removal of sin centers in Jesus Christ, who "is the propitiation for our sins; and not for ours only, but also for the whole world" (ii, 2). He brings to the knowledge and within the reach of man the potent means by which sin is covered, blotted out, taken away; and such an effectual doing away with sin as the work of the devil is inseparably associated in John's thought with *purification* from sin. He who embraces the Christian's hope "purifieth himself even as God is pure" (iii, 3). A new and heavenly life is begotten through this divine propitiation, so that continuance in sin becomes utterly incompatible with the soul thus purified. For "whosoever is begotten of God doeth no sin, because his seed (that is, God's seed, the germ of heavenly life imparted ἄνωθεν, *from above*, John iii, 3) abideth in him: and he cannot sin because he is begotten of God" (iii, 9). The obstacle in the way of bringing the sinner into fellowship with God is the essential opposition of sin and holiness. This epistle emphasizes it as the contrast of light and darkness. "God is light, and in him is no darkness at all." If

PURIFICATION FROM SIN.   87

sinful man come into this light of God, and see and know and love the God of light, *he cannot go on walking in darkness*. He must become a child of the light. "If we walk in the light, as he is in the light, we have fellowship one with another, and the blood of Jesus his Son cleanseth us from all sin" (i, 5-7). The difficulty, accordingly, in the way of reconciliation between sinful man and God is not some imaginary exigency of divine government, but the fact of sin in man. This fact, however, is a breach of the divine order of life, and in that sense may be conceived as rebellion against God's rule. Righteousness and love alike require that this rebellion cease. No change is required in God. He is essentially unchangeable in love and truth and fidelity and righteousness. But "if we say that we have no sin, we deceive ourselves, and the truth is not in us. If we confess our sins, he is faithful and righteous ($\pi\iota\sigma\tau\grave{o}\varsigma$ $\kappa\alpha\grave{\iota}$ $\delta\acute{\iota}\kappa\alpha\iota o\varsigma$) to forgive us our sins, and to cleanse us from all unrighteousness" (i, 8, 9). Herein we discern the origin, the means, the process, and the result of Christ's "propitiation for our sins."

No faithful exposition of these texts can separate them from the imagery of Old Testament offerings of blood for the remission of sin. It is "the blood of Jesus Christ his Son" which is recognized as in some power- *Old Testament imagery of blood offerings.* ful way efficient for the purification of the sinner from all unrighteousness. The sinner has no means or resources within himself to effect a cleansing from all

88   THE MEDIATION OF JESUS CHRIST.

sin. His own penitence and confession of guilt have in them no cleansing power. There must come to his rescue some mediatorial ministry from a source higher than himself; the mediation must involve sacrifice of sufficient significance and worth to affect both God and man, and it should fulfill all those ideals of propitiation, expiation, removal of sin, reconciliation with God, atonement, and satisfaction which are symbolized in offering the blood of life upon an altar to make atonement for the souls of men (Lev. xvii, 11). Such mediatorial propitiation is manifested in the death of Jesus, and "hereby know we love, because he laid down his life for us" (1 John iii, 16). This laying down one's life for others is, as we have already read in John xv, 13, the greatest possible manifestation of love.

This manifestation of love in the person and ministry of the Son of God has an abiding value in the propitiation for our sins. For Jesus is conceived as *The living Paraclete.* now in actual living intercession with the Father, and thus his presence before God in the heavens is a perpetual ministry of reconciliation. "And if any man sin we have an Advocate (παράκλητον, *Comforter, Helper,* sympathetic and cooperative Intercessor) with the Father, Jesus Christ the righteous" (ii, 1). The concept of the holy and righteous Advocate ever living and making intercession for sinners (comp. Isa. liii, 12; Rom. viii, 34; Heb. vii, 25) helps us in the interpretation of all the scriptures which refer to his work of media-

JESUS A PARACLETE.

tion and atonement. We are not to press to a literal significance every metaphorical suggestion of such terms as expiation, intercession, and propitiation; but we do recognize in them all, as employed by the New Testament writers, a true and profound conception of the saving work of Jesus Christ. He is the bleeding sacrifice, the righteous friend and comforter, the interceding advocate and mediator between God and man, and by being all this and more he ever abides as a "propitiation for our sins." But all this ministry of atonement is of no avail for us except "we confess our sins" and "walk in the light" of God.

It is noticeable that in this epistle Jesus Christ is set forth as Paraclete, while in the Fourth Gospel the Paraclete is the Holy Spirit, whom the Father sends in the name of the Son. The peculiar office and work of the Holy Spirit demands its own separate treatment, as showing the abiding and continuous operation of the heavenly ministrations of saving grace. Jesus Christ has finished the work given him to do in the flesh, but as the effective Paraclete he continues the same immanent Saviour of the world. This subject will receive a special discussion near the close of this treatise. But we cannot complete our study of Christ's mediation as found in this epistle without giving attention to the somewhat obscure passage in v, 6-8. The best accredited text may be thus literally translated: "This is he who came through ($διά$) water and blood, Jesus Christ; not in ($ἐν$) the water only, but in the water and in the blood. And

Coming "through water and blood."

the Spirit is that which is bearing witness, because the Spirit is the truth. Because three are they who bear witness, the Spirit and the water and the blood, and the three agree in one" (εἰς τὸ ἕν εἰσιν, *are* directed *toward the one thing;* that is, unite in one and the same testimony). There is no sufficient reason for supposing that the coming through water and blood refers to the "blood and water" which came out of Jesus' side when he was pierced by the spear of the soldier (John xix, 34); for that incidental fact, mentioned only in the Fourth Gospel, cannot be shown to have been any important feature of the Saviour's coming. The reference of the words to the sacraments of baptism and the Lord's Supper is also untenable; for the aorist tense of the verb *came* (ἐλθών) points to a definite historical fact in the past, and it is not true that he came or comes through the sacraments. The sacraments, moreover, are institutions for acknowledging covenant relations and for perpetuating the memory of Christ's death, and are not in any proper sense the accompaniment or means of his coming. And if the writer intended to refer to the two sacraments he should have employed terms more specific than the mere words "water" and "blood;" for while water may suggest baptism, the single word "blood" is not sufficient to indicate the Lord's Supper, in which the bread is as conspicuous as the wine.

A satisfactory explanation of these words requires that we point out two conspicuous facts in the incarnate life of Jesus which may properly be designated by the phrases "through water and blood" and "in the water and in the blood." And there are two signal events, one at the beginning and the other at the end of his public career, which most obviously answer to the expressions "water" and "blood" as here employed. Those events were his baptism in the water of the Jordan and his bloody death upon the cross. This exposition satisfies the requirements of the language, and is confirmed by the analogous statement of Heb. ix, 12, that Christ came near (παραγενόμενος) "through his own blood, and entered once for all into the holy place, having obtained eternal redemption." The water of his baptism and the blood of his cross mark two distinctive crises in the mediatorial ministry of Jesus, and a special emphasis is put upon the blood by the more definite formal repetition: "Not in the water only, but in the water and in the blood;" and the change in prepositions employed (ἐν after διά)[1] serves to indicate that the baptism and the cross were not only means through which, but also conditions in the bounds and elements of which, he came into the world to be a propitiation for our sins. But this more definite statement not only presents an additional form of conceiving the two great events referred to, but seems intended also to controvert the heresy of Cerinthus, who maintained, according to Irenæus,[2] that the Christly nature came

His baptism and his cross.

---

[1] Compare a similar use of the prepositions ἐν and διά in 2 Cor. vi, 4-8.

[2] *Against Heresies*, chap. xxvi, 1.

upon Jesus at his baptism but withdrew from him before he suffered on the cross.

The testimony of the Spirit as stated in verses 6-8 gives peculiar interest to this whole passage, and sup-
plements the idea of the continuous heavenly ministry of Jesus Christ the righteous as our Advocate with the Father already noticed (ii, 1). Along with these notable facts of the water and the blood we have also the abiding witness of the Spirit; and this fact is of the greatest possible value in the case, "because the Spirit is the truth," even as the Christ himself claims to be in John xiv, 6. Accordingly, no one of these great facts stands apart by itself, but all combine in threefold testimony to the saving ministry of Jesus; "for there are three who bear witness, the Spirit and the water and the blood, and the three agree in one." The Spirit is here assigned the precedence, and instead of the neuter the masculine form ($\tau\rho\epsilon\tilde{\iota}\varsigma$) of the numeral is used, as if the writer's thought was mainly on the personal Paraclete, somehow identical with the Christ himself (ii, 1), whose living presence gives perpetual efficacy to the water and the blood. All this united testimony witnesses to the great central truth, stated in v, 11, but which is in fact the burden of the whole epistle: "God gave unto us eternal life, and this life is in his Son." His coming through water and blood was the manifestation of the mystery of the ages, to which the Spirit of truth is ever pointing.[1]

Testimony of the Spirit.

---

[1] So in substance Huther: "By means of the witness of the

DOCTRINE OF JOHN'S APOCALYPSE. 93

The doctrine of John's Apocalypse is equally positive and unmistakable in presenting the saving work of Jesus Christ under the figures of atonement by means of the shedding of blood. In the salutation (i, 5) he is called the one "who loves us and loosed us from our sins by his blood," and in i, 18, he declares himself the living one, who "was dead, and behold, I am alive for the ages of the ages." More than a score of times in this Apocalypse he is called "the Lamb." The Greek word employed is not ἀμνός (as in John i, 29, 36), but ἀρνίον, *little lamb*. A very suggestive passage is that in v, 1-6, where we read that, when no one could be found in heaven or on earth or under the earth able to open the sealed book, it was said that "the Lion who is of the tribe of Judah, the Root of David," would open the book; and when the seer looked to see the mighty Lion come forward, he beheld "a little lamb standing as though it had been slain." But though the diminutive form of the word for *lamb* may suggest something small or feeble, the picture of this Lamb by the throne is otherwise portrayed so as to suggest the highest power and wisdom. He has seven horns and seven eyes, "which are the seven Spirits of God, sent forth into all the earth," and he was worshiped in the songs of heaven as the Lamb "who was

---

Spirit the whole redemptive life of Christ is permanently present, so that the baptism and death of Jesus, although belonging to the past, prove him constantly to be the Messiah who makes atonement for the world."—Meyer, *Critical and Exegetical Handbook*, *in loco*.

slain and who purchased unto God with his blood men out of every tribe and tongue and people and nation" (verse 9). In vii, 14, the glorified multitudes of heaven are described as those who "washed their robes and made them white in the blood of the Lamb." In all these allusions, and others like them which appear in later portions of the book, there is unquestionable reference to sacrificial ideas of the blood of atonement.[1]

---

[1] It is an error, however, of some interpreters to find in the "garment sprinkled with blood," in xix, 13, an allusion to the blood of expiation or atonement. There we have the figure of a conquering hero, drawn from Isa. lxiii, 1-6, and the blood which stains his apparel is not his own blood, but that of his enemies whom he tramples down in the fierceness of his wrath.

CHAPTER VIII.

DOCTRINE OF PETER.

THE early teaching of Peter, as recorded in the Acts of the Apostles, makes prominent the provision for remission of sins in the name of Jesus Christ (Acts ii, 38; iii, 26; iv, 10-12; v, 31; x, 43). The emphasis placed on "the name of Jesus Christ," and on his work as Saviour from sin, can be satisfactorily explained only in the light of his mediatorial office and work as set forth in other scriptures. How else shall one interpret the strong words of Acts iv, 12: "In none other is there salvation: for there is not another name under heaven, that is given among men, wherein we must be saved"? If this teaching of Peter stood alone, unsupported and unexplained by other apostolic preaching, we might not cite these fragments of his sermons as conclusive proof that current ideas of the expiation of sin entered into his conception of the saving work of Christ. Nor are we to suppose that this apostle's doctrinal views of the death of Christ were fully developed at the time he spoke the words recorded in the Acts. But we find upon further inquiry that he, as well as the other apostles, recognized from the first that Christ had made an atonement for sin. The preaching of Philip (Acts viii, 35), based upon Isa.

Teaching of Peter.

liii, 7, 8, set forth Jesus in the figure of a sheep that is led to the slaughter, and would most naturally have explained that same scripture in the light of sacrificial offerings of blood to one who had come from Ethiopia to Jerusalem to worship.

Passing to the First Epistle of Peter, we observe in the salutation (i, 2) an allusion to the "sprinkling of the blood of Jesus Christ," and in verses 18 and 19 of the same chapter we read: "Ye were redeemed, not with corruptible things, with silver or gold, from your vain manner of life handed down from your fathers; but with precious blood of Christ, as of a lamb without blemish and without spot." No faithful exegesis of this scripture can fail to recognize the obvious allusion to such atonement as was wont to be made by the blood of sacrificial lambs. A comparison of the phrase "without blemish and without spot" with the requirements of sacrificial offerings in the law of Exod. xii, 5; Lev. xxii, 19-21; Deut. xvii, 1, puts this beyond all reasonable question. How could a Jew like Peter or any other of his time conceive redemption from sin by means of blood except in the light of that doctrine of vicarious blood of life enunciated in Lev. xvii, 11, and so familiar in the ritual of Jewish worship? The entire passage is one of the most explicit on record for showing the propitiatory character of the death of Jesus Christ.

In 1 Pet. ii, 21-24, the mediatorial sufferings of Christ are further set forth in language which has

VICARIOUS SUFFERING. 97

obvious allusion to the Servant of Jehovah as described in Isa. liii, 4-9: "Christ suffered for you, leaving you an example, that ye should follow his steps: who did no sin, neither was guile found in his mouth: who, when he was reviled, reviled not again; when he suffered, threatened not; but committed himself to him that judgeth righteously: who his own self bare our sins in his body upon the tree, that we, having died unto sin, might live unto righteousness; by whose stripes ye were healed." The statement that he "carried our sins in his body up to the tree" (ἀνήνεγκεν ἐπὶ τὸ ξύλον, *up to and on the tree*) conveys the idea that somehow our sins were crucified upon his cross. The thought is not that of bearing sins up to an altar and placing them thereon; for the cross was in no true sense an altar, nor can we think of sins as an offering upon an altar; but rather he carried the burden of our sins upon his soul up to the cross and nailed it with himself thereon. His soul was thus made an offering for sin (comp. Isa. liii, 10), and by his personal suffering and sacrifice we obtain remission of guilt and the power of living unto righteousness. But this vicarious suffering was no fictitious *quid pro quo*, no mechanical or commercial payment of a debt, no infinite equivalent for an inconceivable infinite demerit.[1] It was rather a mighty mediatorial struggle

---

[1] The theory that the sins of the world were imputed to Christ, or that the guilt of sin was thus imputed, and that he was *punished* for the same with an infliction of suffering and death equal in penal value to all the woe that must have come upon the guilty world, and that all this was necessary to satisfy the de-

even unto death, the death of the cross, whereby we, "having died unto sins," that is, having broken with sin and having become separate from its power by faith in the passion of our Lord, and by an intense sympathetic fellowship in his sufferings, "might live unto righteousness." And so again, to use Isaiah's words (liii, 5), "by his bruise ye were healed."[1] In this respect there is a vicarious element in the sufferings of Christ, and in his bearing our sins up to the cross, which is no example for us, and cannot be.

But while some aspects of Christ's sufferings place him apart from other men, and render his the only

Partaking in Christ's sufferings. name under heaven by which we may be saved, there is another point of view from which it appears that all who suffer for Christ's sake are partakers of his sufferings. We are told in 1 Pet. iii, 17, 18, that it is praiseworthy to suffer in the will of God for welldoing, "because Christ also suffered for sins once, the righteous for the unrighteous, that he might bring us to God." In iv, 1, we also read: "Forasmuch then as Christ suffered

---

mands of justice in the nature of God, may now be treated as obsolete. The theory of full penal satisfaction made by Christ is logically at the basis of the Romish doctrine of indulgences and the later forms of Antinomianism. If Christ has truly paid all the penalty, divine justice can have no further claim on anyone for whom Christ died. A righteous God cannot exact his claims twice over. The theory of penal satisfaction, moreover, logically excludes grace. Where an obligation has been fully discharged, there is nothing left to pardon. See above, p. 71.

[1] *Healing* is to be taken here in the sense of cure and restoration from sin as a fearful disease. Comp. the figure in Isa. vi, 10; Jer. iii, 22; Hos. xiv, 5.

as to the flesh, arm yourselves with the same mind, for he that hath suffered in the flesh hath ceased from sin." The writer's thought is here turned to the more ordinary sufferings of our fleshly human nature in its struggle with temptations to sin. He who suffers in his struggle to overcome sin, and steadfastly refuses to yield to its power as Jesus did in the days of his flesh, "hath ceased from sin," that is, has utterly broken with it and ceased from its control. The brethren, therefore, who are exposed to fiery trial, are exhorted to rejoice in the thought that they are thus made "partakers of Christ's sufferings" (iv, 13). The writer of this epistle was himself "a witness of the sufferings of Christ" (v, 1), and he had confidence that he and all who followed the divine Master should also be partakers of the heavenly glory that was to be revealed; but Christ alone could be spoken of as "a lamb without blemish," whose precious blood makes expiation for the sins of men.

CHAPTER IX.

DOCTRINE OF THE PAULINE EPISTLES.

IN the Pauline epistles we find the mediatorial work of Christ set forth as the very substance of the Gospel.

Teaching of Paul.

The few allusions to the doctrine in Paul's preaching, as recorded in the Acts, accord also with the teaching of the epistles. Thus he proclaims, at Antioch of Pisidia, remission of sins and justification through the crucified and risen Jesus (xiii, 38, 39); at Athens he declares that "it was necessary for the Christ to suffer and to rise again from the dead" (xvii, 3); at Miletus he enjoins the elders of the church "to feed the church of the Lord which he purchased with his own blood" (xx, 28). In 1 Thess. i, 10, Jesus is mentioned as the one "who delivers[1] us from the wrath to come," and in v, 10, as our Lord "who died for us, that, whether we wake or sleep, we should live together with him." Such incidental allusions imply a well-defined doctrine of the saving work of Christ.

The Corinthian epistles contain numerous allusions of a similar character, but do not attempt any elaborate treatment of the doctrine of the cross.

Corinthian epistles.

In proclaiming at Corinth the mystery

---

[1] Compare *the deliverer*, τὸν ῥυόμενον, of this text with the same word in Rom. xi, 26.

or the testimony[1] of God, Paul made "Jesus and him crucified" his great central theme (1 Cor. ii, 2). He held "the word of the cross" to be "the power of God to them that are saved" (i, 18), and that "Christ Jesus was made unto us wisdom from God, and righteousness, and sanctification, and redemption" (i, 30). The Christian believer is "bought with a price" no less or other than the death of the Lord Jesus (vi, 20; vii, 23; viii, 11; xv, 3), who "died for our sins according to the scriptures." It was therefore no new or exceptional idea for this apostle to recognize the bread and cup of the Lord's Supper as a symbol of the communion of the body and of the blood of Christ (x, 16; xi, 25-27), and for him to speak of Christ as our immolated paschal lamb (v, 7). In the light of all these statements it seems impossible to read 2 Cor. v, 14-19, without feeling that the writer is intending to give unmistakable expression to the vicarious nature of the death of Jesus: "The love of Christ constraineth us; because we thus judge, that one died for all, therefore the all died (οἱ πάντες ἀπέθανον); and he died for all, that they who live should no longer live unto themselves, but unto him who died for them and rose again." There is, no doubt, a certain mystical element, peculiar to Paul, in this manner of thinking and speaking (comp. Rom. vi, 5-11; Gal. ii, 20). All who partake of the saving

2 Cor. v, 14-19.

---

[1] There seems little to choose between the two alternative readings μυστήριον and μαρτύριον, both of which are well attested by ancient authorities.

grace of Christ are conceived as crucified and dying along with Christ. In this ideal but spiritually real sense *these all die,* because in fact and truth he died for the sake of all of them (ὑπὲρ πάντων). This entire ministry of saving mercy has its source in God (ἐκ τοῦ θεοῦ, verse 18), "who reconciled us unto himself through Christ, and gave unto us the ministry of reconciliation." According to Paul, all men are by the depraved tendencies of their nature and by their persistent habits of transgression at enmity toward God, but from the bosom of God, as from a fountain of infinite love, spring the passion and the purpose of restoring the fallen, of redeeming the captives of sin, and of effecting a state of harmony and holy fellowship between himself and man. "The ministry of reconciliation" is the mediatorial work of Christ, who died for all, and its magnitude and scope are set forth in most impressive words: "God was in Christ reconciling the world unto himself, not reckoning unto them their trespasses." The object sought in this ministry of reconciliation is the whole world (κόσμον). Nothing less than this could satisfy the yearnings of infinite love, and no more profound or suggestive statement bearing on the doctrine of redemption can be found than finds expression in the words, "God was in Christ reconciling the world to himself." It may well seem

Reconciliation unto God. strange that any exegete should argue, in the face of this statement, that we are to think of God as reconciled to the world rather than the world to God. But it has been maintained that, inasmuch as the Scriptures represent God as a righteous judge, indignant every day with the wickedness of the wicked (Psa. vii, 9-11), and as Paul himself speaks of "the wrath of God against all ungodliness and unrighteousness of men" (Rom. i, 18; comp. Eph. v, 6; Col. iii, 6), the reconciliation here spoken of must needs have reference mainly to the removal of God's wrath against the sinful world. It may be that the controversy is to some extent a vain wrangle over words, for there can be no question as to the attitude of the Holy One toward human sinfulness: he is "of purer eyes than to behold evil, and cannot look on miserable perverseness" (Hab. i, 13). But the question in 2 Cor. v, 18, 19, is not about the essential antagonism of the holiness of God and the sinfulness of the world, but about the object or aim of the reconciliation in Christ; and if the usage of the word καταλλάσσω, *reconcile*, in the New Testament is permitted to have its full weight in deciding the point at issue there ought to be no controversy. In the passage before us the word is employed three times in three successive verses (18-20), and in each case the reconciliation is *unto God,* not of God unto the world, or unto us. The noun καταλλαγή, *reconciliation,* occurring twice in this same passage, in the phrases "the ministry of reconciliation" and "the word of reconciliation," is spoken of as something given and committed unto us, and in the absence of any other reference must be understood as in strict harmony with what the thrice repeated verb affirms—*the reconciliation unto God.*

The use of these same words in Rom. v, 10, 11, is precisely the same: "Being enemies, we *were reconciled to God* through the death of his Son." The reconciliation thus received is affirmed in the most explicit terms to be a reconcilation *unto God* (τῷ θεῷ). The wrath of God against all unrighteousness of men is everywhere and always to be assumed or understood, but what is made conspicuous in Rom. v, 8-11, is not this wrath, but the adorable love of God which provides for the reconciliation of his enemies *unto himself*. The peace between God and the sinner effected by this reconciliation is conceived by Paul as a peace of the sinner *toward God* (πρὸς τὸν θεόν, Rom. v, 1) rather than a peace of God toward the reconciled and justified sinner. The incidental mention of the "reconciliation of the world" in Rom. xi, 15, is in perfect accord with the construction of the word given above, as is also the solemn charge of the apostle, in 1 Cor. vii, 11, that the wife who has improperly departed from her husband ought to be "reconciled to her husband." The wife is the erring party in the case supposed, and, like the sinner, is to be reconciled to the husband. And these are all the instances in the New Testament where the words *katallasso* and *katallage* occur. The intensified form ἀποκαταλλάσσω, which seems designed to add to the shorter word a suggestion of the completeness or thoroughness of the reconciliation, occurs only in Eph. ii, 16, and Col. i, 20, 21, and is in each of these texts employed to express the complete reconciliation *unto God* of those who stood in the relation

THE RECONCILIATION.   105

of aliens and enemies to him. There would seem therefore to be no ground whatever, in the usage of this term, for the idea that it contemplates a reconciliation of God to man. Even the word διαλλάσσω, as employed in Matt. v, 24, shows that the reconciliation enjoined is *toward the injured brother*. The sinner in this case is the one who is about to offer his gift at the altar; he is to go at once and *be reconciled to the brother* who has good reason to complain against him.[1] The injured brother holds toward this offender a relation similar to that which God is supposed to hold toward the sinner in the texts previously cited, and here as there the reconciliation is explicitly spoken of as a reconciliation of the offender to the offended, not of the injured person to the transgressor. This latter may be understood as something necessarily involved in the transaction and sure to follow, but it is not the particular thing affirmed in any of these scriptures.

All these scriptures, however, teach that the reconciliation of the sinner to God is effected through the mediation of Christ, and God and Christ are conceived as one in seeking to bring about this reconciliation. There is nothing in the entire passage of 2 Cor. v, 18-21, which speaks of God as an enemy to be reconciled toward man. There is no allusion to a wrath and hostility toward the sinner on the part of God, but, on the contrary, the whole process of recon-

---

[1] A very different course is prescribed in Matt. xviii, 15, for one who thinks that his brother has sinned against him. In such a situation he is to go after his faulty brother, show him his sin, and seek like God himself to gain him over to the Church.

ciliation originated in him, is mediated through Christ, and proclaimed by the ministers of the word as ambassadors on behalf of Christ.

God originates, Christ mediates, the reconciliation.

It would seem, therefore, a perversion, not to say a caricature, of this scripture to read into it the idea of God standing afar off, filled with sovereign displeasure and hostility toward the world, and only to be appeased and reconciled to man by receiving some satisfactory compensation for offenses against his majesty. The apostle's representation is the most striking opposite of this. God is set forth as entreating and beseeching those who are estranged from him by their trespasses to become reconciled to himself: "As though God were entreating by us, we beseech you on behalf of Christ, be ye reconciled to God."

When now we proceed to inquire into the nature of Christ's mediation in the reconciling of the world to God, we find that he embodies and illustrates by his humiliation and vicarious suffering on account of sin the spirit, the heart, the mind of God. In his saving ministry of reconciliation God is in Christ, not apart from him. Hence the remarkable words that follow in 2 Cor. v, 21: "Him who knew not sin he made sin on our behalf, that we might become the righteousness of God in him." That is, the perfectly sinless Christ, yearning with the emotion of God himself to rescue man from the power of sin, is appointed by God to the task of identifying himself

God in Christ.

2 Cor. v, 21.

MADE SIN FOR US. 107

with humanity so closely as to feel the burden and horror of all its sinfulness. The language is bold and striking, but no more so than Isa. liii, 10, where it is said that Jehovah was pleased to bruise his servant and to make his soul a trespass offering (אָשָׁם; Sept., περὶ ἁμαρτίας). It is not improbable that the apostle had this very passage of Isaiah in his thought. The statement cannot mean that God in any literal or real sense made the sinless one an actual sinner. Many of the older interpreters maintain that the word *sin* is here to be understood in the sense of *sin offering*, and not a little may be said in favor of this explanation.[1] It is much to be preferred over that interpretation which holds that Christ was made to suffer the *punishment* of sin; for the conception of *punishing* the sinless for the sinful, and of imputing guilt to Christ and his personal righteousness to the credit of the guilty transgressor, is a scholastic fiction and abhorrent to the moral sense. But we may understand the apostle here as using the word *sin* in an old pregnant sense for a personal contact with sin, a subjection to suffering and death on account of sin, so real as to be

---

[1] The fact that it is used in the Septuagint of Isa. liii, 10, for אָשָׁם, *trespass offering*, and regularly in the Priest Codex for חַטָּאת, *sin offering* (for example, Exod. xxix, 14, 36; Lev. iv, 3, 8, 20, 32, etc.; Num. vi, 11, 16; vii, 16, 22, etc.), furnishes a strong support for this view. In Ezek. xliii, 25; xlv, 17, 22, and other places it is used in the same sense and construed with ποιέω. The objection that the Septuagint usually has the phrase περὶ ἁμαρτίας is not insuperable. Codexes A and B have εἰς ἁμαρτίαν in Lev. iv, 32. Moreover, the explanation of *sin* in 2 Cor. v, 21, in the sense of *sin-bearer*, is virtually equivalent to what is represented by the sin offering.

mystically conceived as a terrible identification with the sins of the world. The divine purpose of his thus becoming sin for our sake was "that we might become the righteousness of God in him." Here too the word δικαιοσύνη, *righteousness,* is employed in the same bold way as the word *sin* in the previous sentence. The abstract is used for the concrete, and the strange brevity of each expression involves an obscurity in the thought which no exegesis has been able to clear away.

We find a somewhat similar declaration in the Epistle to the Galatians (iii, 13): "Christ redeemed us from the curse of the law, having become in our behalf a curse: for it is written, Cursed is every one that hangeth on a tree: that upon the Gentiles the blessing of Abraham might come in Jesus Christ; that we might receive the promise of the Spirit through faith." In this passage the word *curse,* κατάρα, is emphatic and bears a boldness of expression much like that of *sin* in 2 Cor. v, 21, and it is to be noticed that in both cases the words are used without the article, thus indicating some general character or quality of Christ's redeeming work, and the abstract is used for the concrete to intensify the rhetorical force of the statement. According to Deut. xxi, 22, 23, "a sin worthy of death" was to be punished by putting the criminal to death and hanging his dead body on a tree; but the body was not to be left all night upon the tree, but buried the same day; for, says the Hebrew text, "accursed of God is one that is hanged." Our apostle does not quote accurately either the Hebrew text or the Septuagint, but expresses the main thought in both. The publicly executed criminal was looked upon as an object of God's curse. In a similar manner in verse 10 he quotes another passage from Deut. xxvii, 26, to prove that "as many as are of the works of the law are under curse." That is, all who are conditioned in life by a law of works are under strictest obligation to *observe perfectly all* that the law prescribes and to *continue* in such perfect obedience. Otherwise they fall at once under the curse which the law of Deut. xxvii, 26, pronounces. But the apostle insists that as matter of fact no man is justified before God by way of such perfect continuance in keeping the whole law, and he cites in proof the words of Hab. ii, 4: "The one who is righteous shall live by faith." Here then is a way of salvation by faith, opened by the mediation of Christ, and availing to redeem the Jewish people from the curse which their law imposed on every one who failed to perform all its requirements. The divine purpose of Christ's mediation, however, was not merely the redemption of the Jews from the curse of the law, but that upon the Gentiles also the Gospel preached beforehand unto Abraham (verse 8) might come with its fullness of blessing. Thus it is that both Jews and Gentiles "receive the promise of the Spirit through faith."

In order to accomplish this redemption from the curse of the law Christ "has become a curse for us"

($\unicode{x1F7}\pi\grave{\epsilon}\rho$ $\dot{\eta}\mu\tilde{\omega}\nu$, *on our behalf; for our sake*). The reference to the curse of being hanged on a tree associates most naturally with the thought of Christ nailed upon the cross (comp. 1 Pet. ii, 24; Col. ii, 14). So in Gal. iii, 1, Christ is said to have been "openly set forth crucified." This public and shameful suffering of death had all the outer semblance of the curse of the law, and this open exhibition of Jesus as if he were an accursed criminal was a conspicuous part of his humiliation. It is, perhaps, a little less startling to say he "became a curse on our behalf" than to say that God "made him a sin on our behalf." But both statements are of the nature of metonymy, and cannot be literally understood. Both express the voluntary self-humiliation of Christ and his vicarious identification with man under the curse of sin. He entered into the depths of human suffering and felt most keenly the bitter exposure of sinful man to the curse of violated law, and being himself personally without sin and without any condemnation from law he was the more capable of becoming "greatly amazed and sore troubled" (Mark xiv, 33) over the desperate situation of sin-cursed humanity under the curse of holy law. In all this portraiture of the vicarious suffering of the Redeemer we should look, therefore, to see, not a victim of some extraneous demand of law, but rather a voluntary sympathetic friend of the sinner, the purest embodiment of love as well as of fidelity to truth and righteousness, in whom God's Spirit rules, and whose every action reveals

Christ a curse for our sake.

the mind and feeling of God himself. Hence the peculiar force of the language employed farther on in the epistle (iv, 4, 5): "God sent forth his Son, born of a woman, born under the law, that he might redeem them that were under the law, that we might receive the adoption of sons." _{Gal. iv, 4.}
This redemption from the curse of the law delivers one also from its dominion as a rule of life leading to salvation, so that the newly adopted sons of God are no longer in the position of bondservants, but of sons and heirs, in whose hearts the Spirit cries Abba, Father (verses 6 and 7). Hence, too, the exultant confession of the apostle in vi, 14: "Far be it from me to glory, save in the cross of our Lord Jesus Christ, through whom the world hath been crucified unto me, and I unto the world." Being crucified with Christ he lives in Christ, as we have already heard him say in 2 Cor. v, 14, 15; and in this new and heavenly relationship there is no more curse of legal condemnation, but marvelous salvation from sin. Hence the mystical but characteristic Pauline confession of faith (Gal. ii, 19, 20): "Through law I died to law, that I might live to God. _{Gal. ii, 19, 20.}
With Christ have I been crucified; and it is no longer I that live, but Christ liveth in me; and that which I now live in the flesh I live in faith, namely, that of the Son of God who loved me and gave himself up on my behalf." These words suggest how God is truly in Christ reconciling the world unto himself. The **Lord Jesus Christ "gave himself for our sins, that he**

might deliver us out of this present evil world according to the will of our God and Father" (i, 4). Thus this epistle furnishes a most valuable contribution to the doctrine of the mediation of Christ.

Paul's Epistle to the Romans is usually regarded as his masterpiece for the exposition of Christ's media-

Epistle to the Romans.

torial work in the salvation of men. His great theme is the gospel considered as the "power of God unto salvation to every one that believeth" (i, 16). After a very full showing that all the world of mankind is under condemnation before God on account of a universal sinfulness he makes in iii, 21-26, one of the most formal and comprehensive statements in the New Testament touching the redemption from sin which is effected by the grace of God in Jesus Christ. The passage may be quite literally translated as follows: "But now apart from

Rom. iii, 21-26.

law a righteousness of God has been manifested, being witnessed by the law and the prophets; even the righteousness of God through faith of Jesus Christ[1] unto all them that believe; for there is no distinction; for all sinned and fall short of the glory of God; being justified freely by his grace through the redemption that is in Christ Jesus: whom God set forth as a mercy seat[2] through

---
[1] Genitive of the object: faith that takes hold on Jesus Christ. So too, in verse 26, "he who is of the faith of Jesus" is the one who has faith in Jesus, and believes unto salvation.

[2] ἱλαστήριον, *mercy seat*. Here used without the article, as is the word *Son* in Heb. i, 2 (ἐν υἱῷ), because the *nature, relative quality,* or *symbolic import* of the term is uppermost. This word occurs elsewhere in the New Testament only in Heb. ix, 5, where the

THE REDEMPTION IN CHRIST. 113

faith in his blood, for a showing of his righteousness because of the passing over of the sins done aforetime in the forbearance of God; for the showing of his righteousness in the present time, that he himself might be just and the justifier of him who is of the faith of Jesus."

There are numerous contrasted phrases and minute shades of thought suggested in this passage which it is scarcely the province of dogmatics to expound. Our aim must be to set forth as clearly as possible the apostle's conception of "the redemption that is in Christ Jesus," and the manner by which it becomes effective in showing forth the *The redemption in Christ.* righteousness and grace of God and in securing the forgiveness and justification of the sinner. With this object in view we must study carefully the import of the more striking words and phrases of the text.

1. We observe first that Paul does not regard his teaching here as something new and original with himself, but as a truth which is "witnessed by the law and the prophets;" for he *Not a new teaching.* cites the law, the prophets, and the psalms throughout the epistle to confirm his doctrine (comp. i, 17; iii, 10; iv, 3-8; ix, 25-33). We understand it, however, as Paul's exposition, the way in which this gospel of God was revealed in his conscious experience and thought (comp. Gal. i, 11-17). It accordingly bears the peculiarities of a gospel according to Paul.

---

writer is specifying the different articles of furniture in the holy places of the tabernacle.

114   THE MEDIATION OF JESUS CHRIST.

2. According to Paul's gospel the entire work of redemption in Christ originates with God, so that
<small>Originates with God.</small> whatever Christ does God does; and "the redemption which is in Christ" is a manifestation [1] both of the righteousness and the free grace of God. Justice and love divine thus "meet and kiss each other" in this manifestation of God. Hence it follows that God may be shown to be righteous and to be at the same time a justifier of the man who has faith in Jesus Christ.

3. This demonstrable proof of the righteousness of God explains also his forbearance in passing over the
<small>Passing over former sins.</small> sins which had been committed in the times previous to the appearing of Christ. His righteousness and grace were never wanting, and were never separate from his eternal purpose in Christ (comp. Eph. iii, 11), but his forbearing mercy overlooked times and conditions of ignorance (comp. Acts xvii, 30). This, however, is not to be understood or construed as inconsistent with the fact that "the wrath of God is also revealed from heaven against all ungodliness and unrighteousness of

---

[1] Two Greek words are employed in this passage to express the idea of *manifestation*, φανέρωσις and ἔνδειξις. The former seems to point to an outward sensible exhibition, which anyone so disposed may look upon, and so it differs from ἀποκάλυψις, *revelation*, which is a disclosure made subjectively to the individual soul. A manifestation, however, perceptible to all, may be the outcome of a series of revelations witnessed by prophets of God. The word ἔνδειξις, on the other hand, conveys the idea of a public *demonstration*, an evidential showing forth of some great fact or truth. Both ideas unite in the προέθετο of verse 25: *whom God set forth*, etc.

THE REDEMPTION IN CHRIST. 115

men who restrain the truth in unrighteousness" (Rom. i, 18), but it is a vindication of his love and justice in all the ages of human history. What, therefore, finds an open demonstration in the manifestation of the historical Christ "in the present time" is essentially true for all times, and furnishes our only theodicy of the divine administration of the moral world.

4. There are two Greek words in this passage which must necessarily have great significance in the apostle's doctrine of the mediation of Christ between God and man. They are ἀπολύτρωσις, in verse 24, and ἱλαστήριον, in verse 25. The first means *redemption* in the sense of deliverance from some condition of bondage, and does not differ in any essential or important manner from the main signification of the word λύτρον, *ransom*, which we have already considered in connection with the teaching of Jesus (page 68).[1] Jesus offered his life "a ransom for many" (Mark x, 45), and that self-sacrifice provided for the redemption of the many. "The redemption that is in Christ Jesus" is the divine power in his person and work by the efficiency of which the sinner may be delivered

_{Two Greek words.}

_{λύτρωσις.}

---

[1] For the convenience of the reader disposed to examine all the passages in the New Testament where λυτρόω and its compounds occur we subjoin the following: The verb λυτρόω only in Luke xxiv, 21; Titus ii, 14; 1 Pet. i, 18; λύτρον only in Matt. xx, 28; Mark x, 45; λύτρωσις in Luke i, 68; ii, 38; Heb. ix, 12; λυτρωτής in Acts vii, 35; ἀντίλυτρον in 1 Tim. ii, 6; ἀπολύτρωσις in Luke xxi, 28; Rom. iii, 24; viii, 23; 1 Cor. i, 30; Eph. i, 7, 14; iv, 30; Col. i, 14; Heb. ix, 15; xi, 35. At the root of all these words is λύω, to *loosen*, or *set free*.

from his sins. It is *through this redemption* that he "is justified freely by his grace." In all this more elaborate statement, however, we find thus far no essential thought which we have not already obtained from the simpler declaration of Mark x, 45, that Jesus "came to give his life a ransom for many."

But the word ἱλαστήριον seems designed to direct the reader to a more definite conception of "the re-

ἱλαστήριον.

demption which is in Christ Jesus," and may be regarded as a concrete figurative illustration of ἡ ἀπολύτρωσις, *the redemption*. Here we meet with one of those niceties of biblical exegesis which is of sufficient importance to be studied with much patience and care. Four distinct interpretations have been put upon this word, which may be fairly represented by the Latin terms, *propitiator, propitiatorium sacrificium, propitiatio,* and *propitiatorium*.[1] The distinctive thought in each of these terms may be expressed by the corresponding Greek words ἱλαστής, ἱλαστήριον θῦμα, ἱλασμός, and ἱλαστήριον, and in English by *propitiator, propitiatory sacrifice, propitiation,* and *propitiatory*, this last word in the concrete sense of place or instrument of propitiation. Of these different interpretations it is safe to say that the first named has too little in its favor to deserve extended notice. If the writer intended a personal reference to Christ as a *propitiator* he should have used the word

---

[1] The three forms *propitiator, propitiatio,* and *propitiatorium* are actually found in the different manuscripts of the Latin versions of the New Testament.

PROPITIATORY SACRIFICE. 117

ἱλαστής, and not the neuter form ἱλαστήριον. The second interpretation, which supplies the word θῦμα, *sacrifice,* or else maintains that, as a neuter substantive, ἱλαστήριον without any additional word like θῦμα understood here means *propitiatory sacrifice,* has been adopted by a goodly number of distinguished expositors.[1] The meaning then is that God has exhibited Jesus Christ conspicuously as a propitiatory offering for the sins of men. Against this interpretation there are several weighty objections: (1) The word does not appear to be elsewhere (unless very rarely) employed in this meaning.[2] If the writer wished to express the thought of sacrificial offering he ought by all means to have added the word θῦμα, or some equivalent. (2) It is incongruous with New Testament thought and teaching to speak of God setting forth his Son Jesus Christ as a propitiatory sacrifice. As such an offering Christ rather *presented himself unto God* (Eph. v, 2; Heb. vii, 27; ix, 14, 26, 28; comp. John xvii, 19. (3) The phrase *in his own blood* would be superfluous and tautological if the preceding ἱλαστήριον meant an expiatory sacrifice.

Propitiatory sacrifice.

The Authorized and Revised English Versions of

---

[1] So De Wette, Fritzsche, Meyer, Alford, Jowett, Hodge, Wordsworth, Conybeare, and Howson.

[2] Dion Chrysostom (*Orat.* xi, 1) and Nonnus (*Dionysiaca* xiii) are cited by Meyer and others as sustaining the meaning of sacrificial offerings. Also 4 Macc. xvii, 22, where, however, Swete (*Sept. in loco*) reads διὰ ... τοῦ ἱλαστηρίου θανάτου αὐτῶν, *through their propitiatory death.* Here the word is masculine and an adjective qualifying *death,* and hence not a parallel example.

the New Testament translate the word by the abstract

Propitiation. term *propitiation,* thus following most copies of the Vulgate. This interpretation may construe ἱλαστήριον as a neuter noun in the sense of *means of propitiation,* or it may construe ἱλαστήριον as an adjective in the accusative masculine and as a predicate of ὅν, *whom.* Thus the margin of the Revised Version has it, *whom God set forth to be propitiatory.* Against the first construction lies the fact that the word is found nowhere else as a neuter in the abstract and general meaning of *propitiation.* No other example is adduced in which ἱλαστήριον appears as equivalent or synonymous with ἱλασμός. If the writer desired or intended to say *propitiation,* why did he not employ the unequivocal word which is so rendered in all versions of 1 John ii, 2, and iv, 10? Against the construction which makes it a masculine adjective qualifying ὅν, *whom,* and explains it as descriptive of a personal element in Christ, it may be urged (1) that the adjective is nowhere else applied to persons; (2) that in the examples adduced the object to which it is applied follows the adjective;[1] and (3) it is an uncouth and unexampled assertion to say that "God set forth Christ propitiatory," or "to be propitiatory." God has indeed sent forth and set forth his Son as a manifold revelation of himself in the Christ, but not as propitiatory to himself. So far as

---

[1] The examples often cited are ἱλαστήριον μνῆμα (Josephus, *Ant.* xvi, 7, 1) and ἱλαστηρίου θανάτου (4 Macc, xvii, 22), already cited above.

A MERCY SEAT. 119

he is a sacrifice unto God he offered himself by the sacrifice of himself. Otherwise conceived, there is needless confusion of thought.

We prefer that interpretation of ἱλαστήριον in this text which accords the word the meaning which it bears everywhere else in the biblical Greek, and which has the support of the ancient Greek commentators and a large number of the ablest exegetes of modern times.[1] In the only other place where it occurs in the New Testament (Heb. ix, 5) it designates the "mercy seat," the lid or cover of the ark. This cover was the most central and sacred article of furniture in the holy of holies in the tabernacle. According to Exod. xxv, 17-22, it was made of pure gold, and two cherubim were wrought into the same piece, one at each end, with their wings spread out over the mercy seat and their faces toward it and toward one another. This golden lid covered the two tables of "the testimony" which were placed within the ark, and there, "from above the mercy seat," Jehovah promised to meet and commune with Moses. Into this place the high priest entered alone, once in the year, and sprinkled the mercy seat with blood, "to make atonement (לְכַפֵּר, Sept., ἐξιλάσκεσθαι) for the children of Israel." The slab of gold thus fitted to cover the top of the ark was called in the Hebrew

Mercy seat.

---

[1] So Origen, Chrysostom, Theodoret, Cyril, Theophylact, Erasmus, Luther, Calvin, Grotius, Olshausen, Philippi, Tholuck, Umbreit, Liddon, Gifford (in *Speaker's Commentary*), Lange, Cremer (*Bibl.-Theol. Lex.*), Ritschl (*Rechtfertigung und Versohnung*, vol. ii, p. 169).

הַכַּפֹּרֶת, *the cap'poreth*, and this word is everywhere translated in the Septuagint by ἱλαστήριον. In Exod. xxv, 16 (17), where the word first appears, this Greek version reads: "Thou shalt make a propitiatory cover of pure gold" (ἱλαστήριον ἐπίθεμα χρυσίου καθαροῦ).[1] Elsewhere throughout the Septuagint כַּפֹּרֶת is uniformly translated by ἱλαστήριον, without any further defining word. In view of these facts it is difficult to suppose that Paul would have employed a Greek word so familiar to all readers of the common version of the Old Testament in any other meaning than that which it bears in that version. The reasons, accordingly, for this meaning of the word in the passage under discussion are the following:

(1) This is the only well-accredited meaning of the word in the biblical Greek.

(2) The mercy seat was the most sacred and solemn symbol connected with the system of Levitical service in the tabernacle and in the temple. It was the secret place of the Most High, the throne of the presence chamber of Jehovah, the God of Israel. In that most holy place he would meet and commune with his people, through their anointed representative.

(3) The symbolical significance of the mercy seat made it a very appropriate figure for the apostle to

---

[1] It may be equally proper to construe the ἐπίθεμα in this exceptional text as in apposition with ἱλαστήριον, and so Gifford actually does: "Thou shalt make a propitiatory, a lid of pure gold." He also observes that this apposition of the two words "is the more natural, because on this first occurrence of כפרת the translators might wish to show that they had both meanings under their consideration."

A MERCY SEAT. 121

use by way of metaphor to illustrate "the redemption that is in Christ Jesus." It is worthy of special note that in Heb. ix, 7-12, immediately following the only other place in the New Testament where ἱλαστήριον occurs, the symbolism of the holy of holies is spoken of as a figure (παραβολή) of the atoning ministry of Christ, who "through his own blood entered in once for all into the holy place, having obtained eternal redemption."[1]

(4) This interpretation best explains the addition of the emphatic phrase *in his blood*. The mercy seat was a golden covering, over which were the faces and wings of the cherubim. It had no propitiatory significance until the priest sprinkled it with the blood of atonement. So, in the figure, it is only after Christ has entered the holy place through his own blood that God set him forth as a mercy seat and exhibited the saving mystery of eternal redemption "through faith in his blood." And so it was "that the way into the holy place was not made manifest while the first tabernacle was yet standing" (Heb. ix, 8).

(5) The middle voice employed in the Greek verb προέθετο, *set forth for himself*, also comports with this interpretation of ἱλαστήριον. It indicates God's own personal interest and participation in the redemption which is in Christ, and in the consequent "showing forth of his righteousness." God openly set forth in his own interest his Son Jesus Christ as the reality and

---

[1] On the symbolism of the mercy seat, see further my *Biblical Hermeneutics*, p. 272, and *Biblical Apocalyptics*, p. 83.

fulfillment of all that was symbolized by the mercy seat.

Further confirmation of this interpretation will be seen, we think, as we pass under review the various objections that have been raised against it:

(1) Some writers have declared that ἱλαστήριον is an incorrect translation of the Hebrew כפרת. To which it would be sufficient to reply, in view of the facts already adduced, that, whether it be a correct or an incorrect translation, it is the one word uniformly employed in the biblical Greek to represent the *capporeth*, and Paul would not have been likely to make use of it in another or an exceptional meaning. But the truth is that the verb כפר in its intensive form (Piel), and the derivatives of the same, are almost invariably used in the sense of making an atonement for sin; *covering it over* as if putting it out of sight. And this is the obvious significance of the *capporeth* in the holy place. Sprinkled with the blood of atonement it was a perpetual symbol of the divine reconciliation secured thereby. It *covered* "the testimony" of the two tables of law deposited within the ark, and thus proclaimed how mercy covers wrath, and effects the reconciliation of the sinner unto God. And this idea was appropriately set forth by the Greek word ἱλαστήριον, a means and instrument divinely appointed to secure reconciliation between the sinner and his God, and hence it is appropriately translated into English by *mercy seat*.

(2) It has been objected that there is an incon-

gruity in the figure of the blood of a sacrifice and that of a mercy seat. But the incongruity, if any, is one of the objector's own making. The mercy seat as such was not without blood (Lev. xvi, 14; Heb. ix, 7), and the text under discussion affirms explicitly that Christ as a mercy seat effects the redemption by means of his own blood. We have already seen that ἱλαστήριον does not mean a sacrifice, or a propitiatory offering; but its significant symbolism is never apparent apart from the blood which the high priest sprinkled thereon in the day of atonement.

(3) Others object that the idea of mercy seat would be inappropriate in view of the fact that Christ is here said to be set forth "for a showing (ἔνδειξις) of his *righteousness.*" But this objection overlooks the fact that in Paul's thought the grace and the righteousness of God in Christ are never separate. No more emphatic statement appears in this whole passage than that we are *"justified* freely by his grace through the redemption that is in Christ Jesus." Moreover, both grace and righteousness are alike symbolized in the blood-sprinkled cover of "the ark of the covenant."

(4) It is also objected that it would be violently abrupt to introduce such a figure here, without anything in the preceding context preparing the way for it. But this objection seems to forget that the word ἱλαστήριον occurs nowhere else in Paul's writings, and if its well-attested and uniform meaning elsewhere seem abrupt in this connection, how much more out of place would be an exceptional and questionable use of

the word? We believe, on the contrary, that the emphatic mention in the preceding verse of the gracious "redemption that is in Christ Jesus" does prepare the way for this figure of atonement, and the repeated references to "the law," both before and after this verse, assume that the readers of this epistle were familiar with the means and methods of atonement provided in the law.

(5) The last observation may also sufficiently dispose of the objection that such a reference to the *capporeth* would be out of place in an epistle addressed in part to Gentile readers. If this objection were valid, it must also apply to numerous other Old Testament references in the epistle. But Paul's contention throughout this epistle is first and mainly with the Jew, and he may as well have assumed that his first readers would be familiar with the mysteries of the holy place in the tabernacle, as does the author of Heb. ix, 7-14.

(6) But it is urged that Christ is nowhere else in the New Testament presented under the figure of a mercy seat; to which it has been well replied that the same objection may be made to the figure of the brazen serpent (John iii, 14), the baptism unto Moses and the spiritual Rock (1 Cor. x, 2-4), Christ "made sin for us" (2 Cor. v, 21), and "a curse for us" (Gal. iii, 13). And it should also be observed that in the immediate context and argument following the only other mention of the mercy seat in the New Testament (Heb. ix, 5) we read quite an elaborate exposition of the "figure" ($\pi\alpha\rho\alpha\beta o\lambda\acute{\eta}$) of Christ's mediation as seen in

his "entering in once for all into the holy place, through his own blood, and (his thus) obtaining eternal redemption" (verse 12; comp. x, 19, 20).

(7) But the most weighty objection is generally felt to be the absence of the article before ἱλαστήριον. In the somewhat analogous illustration of 1 Cor. v, 7, the language of the apostle is, τὸ πάσχα ἡμῶν ἐτύθη Χριστός, *Our passover* (that is, paschal lamb) *was sacrificed, even Christ*. Here the word *passover* is made definite both by the article and the pronoun, and it would seem to have been certainly proper, if not necessary, to qualify the word *mercy seat* in like manner, had the apostle used ἱλαστήριον in this specific sense.[1] The force of this argument is not to be denied, and it may be admitted that the more general term, *a propitiation*, would have suited the context. Nevertheless, as Schaff says in his additions to Lange's comments, this objection is by no means conclusive. For in expressing the main thought of 1 Cor. v, 7, Paul might truly have said, "Christ was sacrificed as a paschal lamb." This form would have emphasized *his character as a paschal lamb* rather than his being *our* paschal lamb. And so we believe that the absence of the article before ἱλαστήριον gives emphasis to the symbolical character and significance of the word. He was not manifested or set forth as *the mercy seat* of the sanctuary made with hands (comp. Heb. ix, 11), but as a mercy seat which embodied and represented

---

[1] And so Theodoret paraphrases it: "The Lord Christ is the true mercy seat" (τὸ ἀληθινὸν ἱλαστήριον).

all that was ever typified and symbolized in the well-known blood-sprinkled mercy seat of the tabernacle. Furthermore, the two clauses, *through faith* and *in his blood,* which follow and attach immediately to the word ἱλαστήριον, are of such a definitive character as to exclude the article before the word. God set forth Christ not as *the* mercy seat of the old tabernacle, but as *a mercy seat* in which the Christly redemption becomes eternally efficient *through faith in his blood.* These additional words, thus defining and enhancing the saving significance of Christ's priestly mediation, sufficiently account for the absence of the article.

(8) Finally, it has been objected that προέθετο, *set forth,* would not be a suitable word to use in reference to the cover of the ark which was ever kept in the most holy place and hidden from the view of the people. But this objection is thoroughly refuted by the fact that Christ's mediation *makes known* the mystery of the ancient types and symbols. "The way unto the holy place was indeed not made manifest while the first tabernacle remained standing" (Heb. ix, 8); but the veil no longer hides that secret place; we may now enter "with boldness into the holy place by the blood of Jesus" (Heb. x, 19). The great thought in the *setting forth* of Christ as a mercy seat is that God has thus manifested the profound mystery of the most secret and sacred symbol connected with his ancient law and testimony. Every essential truth which is found in the words "propitiation," "reconciliation," and "atonement" is included in Christ's mediation

conceived as the reality of what was symbolized by the mercy seat, and God's setting forth his Son in this light was the consummate revelation of his own glory, grace, and truth.

5. This passage, furthermore, emphasizes the important truth that the righteousness of God manifested in Christ is a blessedness to be realized only "through faith in his blood." The Pauline phrase "righteousness of God" (comp. Rom. i, 17; x, 3; 1 Cor. i, 30; 2 Cor. v, 21; Phil. iii, 9) is to be here understood as a righteousness which in some sense proceeds from God, and it is well-pleasing in his sight when it becomes the actual possession or state of him that believes in Jesus. It is "through the redemption that is in Christ," and "through faith in his blood" that a man may become "freely justified" by the grace of God. Like Abraham, one believes in God and in Christ, and it is reckoned unto him for righteousness (Rom. iv, 3). This doctrine of faith is something that may be verified in human experience. The gracious blessedness is mediated in Jesus Christ and appropriated by personal faith on the part of the believer. God's justice and grace are both magnified in the sacrifice of Jesus. While the first tabernacle stood the way into the holy of holies was hidden from view (Heb. ix, 8), but the blood of Jesus has opened the way into the holy places not made with hands, and exposed to the eye of faith a mercy seat which assures the free and complete pardon of every sinner "who is of the faith of Jesus." In all this divine ministra-

128   THE MEDIATION OF JESUS CHRIST.

tion God and Christ are one, and in the blood of the cross we have an exhibition of the way of salvation that was symbolized by the mercy seat.

6. It is to be noticed that this "righteousness of God," while attainable "apart from law," has in the highest possible manner honored the law. There can be no unrighteousness in the God who judges the world (iii, 5, 6), and his law is essentially holy and righteous and good (vii, 12). The symbolism of the mercy seat forever sets Christ forth as the "end[1] of the law unto righteousness to every one that believeth" (x, 4). The law is not dishonored, but rather enhanced, by the gracious provision of making faith in Christ the regulative principle which leads the believer unto righteousness. "Through the law cometh the knowledge of sin" (iii, 20; vii, 7), for in its inmost nature and essence "the law is spiritual" (vii, 14); that is, it is of the very nature of the Spirit of God. The law, in this deepest sense, is God himself revealing his essen-

Magnifies the law.

---

[1] The word τέλος, *end*, is here to be understood in its ordinary meaning of *termination, conclusion*. Christ has ended the law as a condition and means leading unto righteousness. But, as Philippi has well said, "in a dogmatic point of view, the fact of Christ being the end of the law is no doubt based simply upon the fact that he is the *fulfillment* and *aim* of the law. For either the law itself would ·be without sanction, or its abolition by Christ without reason, if he had abrogated without fulfilling it. On the other hand, the law evinces its own as well as Christ's authority, in the fact that it proposed as its object and aim to come to an end through fulfillment by Christ. It has come to an end, because now, in place of the requirement of works, the requirement of faith is established (vii, 1-6)."—*Commentary on Romans*, x, 4.

HOLY MYSTERY OF GOD. 129

tial holiness and righteousness to the hearts of men (comp. i, 15). But in the symbolism of the mercy seat the claims of this spiritual law, as represented in the "tables of testimony" within the ark and safely guarded there, are seen to be now *covered* and *ended* for him that believes in Jesus; for faith in the blood of Christ, instead of perfect obedience to the law, is reckoned unto him for righteousness.

In this important passage in Romans we thus have in somewhat fuller form, and by means of symbolic illustration, the same truth that we have already studied in the profound statement of 2 Cor. v, 19, that "God was in Christ reconciling the world unto himself." We are not able to derive from either passage a particular theory of atonement. The sublime fact is declared; deep and far-reaching suggestions are put forward; but the holy mystery of God in Christ remains. The redemption in Christ is an exhibit of mysterious necessities of the moral world, and is mediated and becomes efficient unto salvation "through faith in his blood." Sin is shown to be "exceeding sinful" (vii, 13), and in the light of the holy, righteous, good, spiritual law every mouth is stopped and all the world is seen to be under the condemning judgment of God (iii, 19).

<small>Fact and illustration, but no theory.</small>

But according to Paul the redemption that is in Christ is effected and carried on to completion by the resurrection and heavenly life of Jesus as well as by his death on the cross.

<small>Rom. iv, 25.</small>

He says in iv, 25, that he "was delivered up for

our trespasses, and was raised for our justification." In some places it is said that God delivered him up for us (viii, 32) and in others that Christ delivered himself up (Gal. ii, 20; Eph. v, 2; comp. 1 Tim. ii, 6; Titus ii, 14; Matt. xx, 28), but whichever way we state it, his being delivered up unto death was on account of human sinfulness, and his resurrection was equally necessary for the consummation of his mediatorial work. Hence the significance of what is written in v, 8-11: "God commendeth his own love toward us, in that, while we were yet sinners, Christ died for us. Much more then, being now justified in his blood, shall we be saved from the (divine) wrath through him. For if, while we were enemies, we were reconciled to God through the death of his Son, much more, being reconciled, shall we be (continuously) saved in his life; and not only so, but we also glory in God through our Lord Jesus Christ, through whom we have now received the reconciliation." The complete redemption is, accordingly, not only a remission of sins through the mediating death of Jesus, but a continuous and eternal salvation, in which the believer, being reconciled to God, lives the new life of righteousness by faith, and realizes that there is no enmity in his heart toward God, but a glorious state of reconciliation. To the same effect is that which is written in vi, 8-11: "If we died with Christ, we believe that we shall also live with him; knowing that Christ being raised from the dead dieth no more; death no more hath dominion over

Continuous reconciliation.

THE GREAT ANTITHESIS. 131

him. For the death that he died, he died unto sin once for all: but the life that he liveth, he liveth unto God. Even so reckon ye also yourselves to be dead unto sin, but alive unto God in Christ Jesus." This general trend of thought and argument is carried on to the close of chapter viii, where the apostle asks (verse 32), as if in a rapture of emotion: "He that spared not his own Son, but delivered him up for us all, how shall he not also with him freely give us all things?" Again in xiv, 9, he returns to this inspiring thought: "Whether we live or die, we are the Lord's. For to this end Christ died and lived, that he might be Lord of both the dead and the living."

In the great antithesis set forth in v, 12-21, we should observe how the gracious mediation of Christ is made to offset all the consequences of Adam's transgression. "By the trespass of one the many died, but much more did the grace of God, and the gift in the grace of the one man Jesus Christ, abound unto the many" (verse 15). In all these contrasts we note especially the difference in the *kind* of effects resulting from the acts of the two opposite representatives of humanity. Through the one, condemnation and death were imposed upon all men, but through the righteous act of Christ provision is made for the justification of all, so that "where sin abounded, grace did more exceedingly abound, in order that, as sin reigned in death, even so might grace reign through righteousness unto eternal life through Jesus Christ our Lord."

[margin: Great antithesis of v, 12-21.]
[margin: Grace superabounding.]

132   THE MEDIATION OF JESUS CHRIST.

In all these scriptures we may perceive the great thought of iv, 25, that Christ died for our sins, and was raised and ever lives for our justification and eternal life. And so the efficiency of Christ's redeeming work is perpetual. So long as sin and trespass and death continue in Adam's posterity, so long the Christly redeeming grace continuously avails to counteract the evil, and is not therefore to be conceived as a finished work. Because of Adam's trespass, sin abounds and death reigns; because of Christ's redemptive mediation, grace abounds more exceedingly and reigns through righteousness unto eternal life.

So far as the Ephesian and Colossian epistles refer to the mediation of Christ they are in perfect accord with the other Pauline writings. In Eph. i, 6, 7, we read of "the glory of his grace, which he freely bestowed on us in the Beloved, in whom we have redemption in his blood, the forgiveness of our trespasses, according to the riches of his grace." According to ii, 13-16, the Gentiles who "once were far off are made nigh in the blood of Christ," and both Gentile and Jew are happily "reconciled in one body unto God through the cross, having slain the enmity thereby." With great confidence, therefore, the apostle speaks of the love of Christ, who "gave himself up in our behalf, an offering and a sacrifice to God for an odor of a sweet smell" (v, 2). Such an obvious allusion to Old Testament offerings (comp. Exod. xxix, 18; Lev. i, 9, 13, 17) shows be-

SACRIFICE OF HIS LIFE.   133

yond question that the writer had no hesitation in putting forward the sufferings and death of Christ as having something in common with the expiatory sacrifices of the Hebrew ritual. It was the offering up of a spotless life on behalf of the lives of many who were "dead through trespasses" that they might live and walk in light as beloved children of God. *Offering of a spotless life.* Further on (v, 25) it is said that "Christ loved the church and gave himself up on her behalf." Thus we observe that Christ's giving himself up as a sacrifice for the benefit of others is a very familiar Pauline thought (comp. Gal. i, 4; ii, 20; Rom. iv, 25). It is prominent in the great kenotic text (Phil. ii, 5-8) which emphasizes his humbling himself and becoming obedient even unto the death of the cross. It is equally explicit in the Epistle to the Colossians, where we are told that it was the Father's good pleasure "through him to reconcile all things unto himself, having made peace through the blood of his cross" (i, 20). In him, the Son of the Father's love, "we have our redemption, the forgiveness of our sins" (i, 14). So far as Jew and Gentile were guilty of trespasses and felt the condemning power of the law upon their conscience, the death and resurrection of Christ effected complete deliverance. They are conceived as "buried with him in baptism," and "raised with him through faith in the working of God, who raised him from the dead, having forgiven us all our trespasses; having blotted out the bond written in ordinances that was against us, which was contrary to us: and he hath taken it out of the way, nailing it to the cross" (ii, 12-14). The condemning statute of the law hung like a bonded debt over us; but the Lord Jesus took it as he did the burden of all our sins, carried it in his own body upon the cross and nailed it there (comp. 1 Pet. ii, 24). Our faith lays hold with adoring wonder on this vicarious sufferer, so that we become crucified with him, but with him also live again.

The Pastoral Epistles have but few direct references to the doctrine of redemption in Christ, but these confirm the Pauline teaching. In 1 Tim. i, 15, we are admonished how "faithful is the saying, and worthy of all acceptation, that Jesus Christ came into the world to save sinners." In ii, 5, 6, we have the very comprehensive declaration, "There is one God, one mediator also between God and men, himself man,[1] Christ Jesus, who gave himself a ransom

In Pastoral Epistles.

---

[1] Effective mediation between two parties, disparate as God and man, would seem to require the intervention of one who was at once partaker of the nature and secrets of both parties. And this was the peculiar qualification of Christ Jesus, who came into the world as the representative of "the King of the ages, the incorruptible, invisible, only God" (i, 17), and "came to save sinners" (i, 15). To accomplish this redemptive mediation, he must needs be "manifest in the flesh" (iii, 16) in order to reveal the invisible God to men in the flesh, and to give himself a ransom for all. Hence the emphasis here put upon the humanity of the mediator. "The human nature of Christ," says Ellicott, "is specially mentioned as being the state in which his mediatorial office was visibly performed. The omission of the article (before *man*, in ii, 5) must be preserved in translation. In a different context Christ might clearly have been designated as *the man*, 'the representative man of humanity;' here, however, as the apostle only wishes to mark the nature in which Christ acted as mediator, but not any relation in which he stood to that nature, he designedly omits the article."—*Commentary, in loco.*

SALVATION FOR ALL.

for all" (ἀντίλυτρον ὑπὲρ πάντων). The word here translated *ransom* occurs nowhere else in the New Testament, but seems to be intended for a more emphatic form of λύτρον, which is employed in Matt. xx, 28, and Mark x, 45. The meaning is substantially the same in all these texts. The Redeemer is a vicarious sufferer; he freely lays down his life in the place of and on behalf of many. The same truth is also affirmed in Titus ii, 14: "Christ gave himself for us, that he might redeem us (λυτρώσηται ἡμᾶς) from all iniquity, and purify unto himself a people for his own possession, zealous of good works." Thus we are assured that the grace of God brings salvation within reach of all men who deny themselves all ungodliness and live righteously (verses 11 and 12). God and Christ work together in accomplishing this glorious salvation.

Ransom for all.

CHAPTER X.

DOCTRINE OF THE EPISTLE TO THE HEBREWS.

OF all the New Testament writings the Epistle to the Hebrews furnishes the most elaborate discussion of the mediatorial ministry of Christ. In that part of the epistle which we may regard as peculiarly doctrinal (i-x, 18) the Lord Jesus is set forth in several different

Outline of the Epistle. relations, and an outline of the author's argument is in substance as follows: After an introductory paragraph (i, 1-4) in which the Son of God is extolled as heir of all things, maker of the ages, effulgence of God's glory, and very image of his being, upholding all things, effecting purification of sins, and enthroned with the Most High, he proceeds to show (1) that as Son of God he is far above the angels (i, 5-ii, 18); (2) that he is worthy of more glory than Moses and Joshua (iii, 1-iv, 13); (3) that he is a great high priest, superior to Aaron and like Melchizedek (iv, 14-vii, 28); and (4) that he is minister of a more perfect tabernacle and mediator of a better covenant (viii, 1-x, 18). It will be seen upon the very face of this outline how largely the

Large use of Old Testament. writer draws upon the Old Testament for imagery and illustration to enforce his argument. He seems never to forget that he is writing TO HEBREWS. Though Jesus is made for a little time lower than the angels, it is "that by the grace of God he should taste death for every one," and, "having made purification of sins," and "because of the suffering of death," should be "crowned with glory and honor." It was eminently fitting (ἔπρεπεν) that God, "for whom are all things, and through whom are all things, in bringing many sons unto glory, should make the author of their salvation perfect through sufferings" (ii, 9, 10).[1] This princely leader partook of the flesh and blood of the seed of Abraham that he might be truly identified in nature with the children he would save, and "that through death he might bring to naught him that had the power of death, that is, the devil, and might deliver all them who through fear of death were all their lifetime subject to bondage" (ii, 14, 15). He is not laying hold upon angels for the purpose of helping such beings as they are, but upon men of flesh and blood, beset with manifold temptations. It was, accordingly, a matter of obligation and necessity (ὤφειλεν, verse 17) that he should "in all things be made like unto his brethren, that he might become a merciful and faithful high priest in things pertaining to God, to make propitiation (ἱλάσκεσθαι) for the sins of the people." Here for the first time in this epistle Jesus is called "high priest," and it deserves note that the word *propitiate*, profoundly suggestive in its metaphorical allusion to the mercy seat

---

[1] We have no English word that fully represents all that is suggested by ἀρχηγός, here and in xii, 2, rendered *author*. It fairly means one who both *begins and leads on* in some great enterprise.

(ἱλαστήριον, comp. ix, 5; Rom. iii, 25), is employed to designate his priestly work. It is also worthy of note that Jesus is called priest and high priest only in this Epistle to the Hebrews, and here the title of high priest is ascribed to him at least ten times.

Having introduced him (in ii, 17) as "a merciful and faithful high priest," and having further called him in iii, 1, "the apostle and high priest of our confession," he goes on to speak in chapters iii and iv of Christ's superiority to Moses and Joshua, and at iv, 14, returns to this subject of the high-priesthood of "Jesus the Son of God, who has passed through the heavens," and devotes the rest of the epistle mainly to a presentation of his heavenly ministry. Of this superior priest we are told that he is touched with the feeling of our infirmities, tempted in all points as we are, without sin, called and appointed of God, a man who prayed with strong cries and tears, who learned obedience by the things which he suffered, and, having been perfected through suffering, became to all who obey him the author of eternal salvation (iv, 15-v, 9). Psa. cx, 4, is cited and repeated several times (v, 6, 10; vi, 20; vii, 17), and the whole of chapter vii is given to show that Christ is divinely styled "a priest forever after the order of Melchizedek." The superior order or manner of Melchizedek is enhanced in chapter vii by a number of considerations, all well adapted to impress a devout Hebrew of the first Christian century. (1) First, it is pointed out that the

Superior priesthood of Jesus.

Like Melchizedek.

ancient king of Salem, described only in Gen. xiv, 18-20, was both king and priest, and, being without recorded genealogy, and without record of his birth or his death, he remains a priest continually (verses 1-3). (2) His superiority to Abraham and to the sons of Levi is next argued by means of a peculiar rabbinical argument (verses 4-10). (3) Further, if the Levitical priesthood had been perfect, there could have been no reason for another priesthood after the order of Melchizedek rather than of Aaron (verses 11-19). (4) Christ's priesthood, moreover, is confirmed by Jehovah's oath, giving it a majesty unknown to the Levitical priests (verses 20-22). (5) It is also an unchangeable priesthood, for, ever living to make intercession, Christ can have no successor (verses 23-25). (6) Finally, he is sinless, made higher than the heavens, and by the word of the oath perfected forever (verses 26-28).

But the deeper mysteries of his priestly work are to be seen in the symbolism of the tabernacle and the mediatorial ministry of the new covenant in Christ. The Son of God is *Symbolism of the tabernacle.* declared to be the minister of a more perfect tabernacle and the mediator of a better covenant, enacted upon better promises (viii, 1-6), and Jer. xxxi, 31-34, is cited as the word of the Lord in proof of this declaration. The old sanctuary and its holy places and vessels and ordinances of divine service were only "a copy and shadow of the heavenly things" (viii, 5; ix, 9, 23; x, 1), and were destined in the nature of things to grow old and vanish away (viii, 13), giving place to that which is essentially better and more spiritual. As every priest is appointed to offer gifts and sacrifices (viii, 3), so Christ entered once for all into the holy of holies in the heavens (ix, 12, 24), as if sprinkling the heavenly mercy seat with his own blood. He has thus "been once offered to bear the sins of many" (ix, 28); "once at the end of the ages manifested to put away sin by his sacrifice" (ix, 26). This repeated mention of the offering of Christ through his atoning blood "once for all" (comp. vii, 27; ix, 12, 26, 28; x, 10; 1 Pet. iii, 18) has obvious allusion to the well-known law of the Jewish high priest going into the holy of holies "once in the year" (ix, 7; Lev. xvi, 34), and sprinkling the mercy seat with "blood of goats and calves and bulls" (ix, 12, 13; x, 4; comp. Lev. xvi, 14, 15). The entrance of Christ "into heaven itself now to appear before the face of God for us" (ix, 24) has made that presence-chamber a "throne of grace," into which we too may boldly enter by the new and living way which he has dedicated for us in his blood (iv, 16; x, 19-21). Thus has he "obtained eternal redemption" (ix, 12; comp. Rom. iii, 24); "for if the blood of goats and bulls, and the ashes of a heifer sprinkling them that have been defiled, sanctify unto the cleanness of the flesh: how much more shall the blood of Christ, who through the eternal Spirit offered himself without blemish unto God, cleanse your conscience from dead works to serve the living God?" (ix, 13, 14.) All this language with its multiplicity of metaphorical allusion to the places and ordinances of the Levitical sanctuary, and especially to the divine service of the day of atonement, accords strikingly with our exposition of Rom. iii, 24, 25, and goes far to confirm it. Our high priest and minister of the true tabernacle "sat down on the right hand of the throne of the Majesty in the heavens" (viii, 1, 2); his throne is God's throne (i, 8); he is conceived as sprinkling that throne with his own blood, and abiding there forever as a heavenly mercy seat, "manifested to put away sin by the sacrifice of himself."

This manifoldness of metaphorical allusions all centering in the thought of a heavenly high priest, who enters the holy place offering his own blood and abiding thus continually, is also in accord with that interpretation of the difficult passage in ix, 15-18, which recognizes in "the mediator of the new covenant" one who in his own person and work is at once maker, mediator, and sacrificial offering.[1] This fact does not seem to be duly

---

[1] It will be well for the reader to notice the following translations of Heb. ix, 16, 17. The Authorized Version reads: "For where a testament is, there must also of necessity be the death of the testator. For a testament is of force after men are dead: otherwise it is of no strength at all while the testator liveth." The Anglo-American Revision has: "For where a testament is, there must of necessity be the death of him that made it. For a testament is of force where there hath been death (margin, *over the dead*): for doth it ever avail while he that made it liveth?" The American Standard Edition makes the last sentence affirmative instead of interrogative: "For it doth never avail while he that made it liveth." Macknight on the *Apostolical Epistles* translates: "For where a covenant, there is a necessity that the

appreciated by those interpreters who insist that the word διαθήκη must in verses 16 and 17 mean a *testament*, a *will,* or *deed of bequest.* Outside of these two verses the word is used fifteen times in this epistle, always in the sense of *covenant.* Such is its meaning also in every other passage of the New Testament where it occurs, as also in the Septuagint, where it nearly always appears as the representative of the Hebrew בְּרִית. It would seem, therefore, like a harsh and violent procedure in biblical exegesis to import a new meaning of the word in these two verses, and such procedure should be justified only by most decisive reasons.

The following reasons for such a sudden change of meaning have been offered: (1) The language of verses 16 and 17 is exceedingly harsh and unmeaning on retaining the idea of a *covenant;* for (2) διαθέμενος in both these verses can only mean a maker of a will or testament, and not of a sacrificial offering; (3) it is not true that the death of a covenant maker is necessary to make a

Reasons for testament.

---

death of the appointed sacrifices be brought in. For a covenant is firm over dead sacrifices, seeing it never hath force whilst the appointed sacrifice liveth." In a similar way "J. C.," in Adam Clarke's *Commentary:* "For where there is a covenant, it is necessary that the death of the appointed victim should be exhibited; because a covenant is confirmed over dead victims, since it is not at all valid while the appointed victim is alive." He further observes: "Διαθέμενος is not a substantive, but a participle, or a participial adjective, derived from the same root as διαθήκη and must have a substantive understood. I therefore render it the disposed or appointed victim, alluding to the manner of disposing or setting apart the pieces of the victim, when they were going to ratify a covenant."

TESTAMENT OR COVENANT. 143

covenant valid; (4) the mention of "the eternal inheritance" in verse 15 suggests the idea of a will or testamentary document, and so justifies the change in meaning from *covenant* to *testament*. (5) Moreover, the statements of verses 16 and 17 are of the nature of a general well-known custom, and therefore most naturally explained as referring to the fact that the death of a testator is necessary to place his will and deed of bequest beyond question.

These reasons, however, are not satisfactory or conclusive,[1] and whatever relief they may seem to afford in explaining some of the statements of verses 16 and 17, they leave other statements without a clear interpretation. Difficulties present themselves on any exposition, and our search should be for that view of the passage which best satisfies all the demands of the writer's argument. Over against the reasons given for translating διαθήκη *testament* we may say (1) that the word appears to have that meaning nowhere else in biblical Greek; (2) that the context is very much against it: διαθήκη is the main word in the passage, and the "new covenant" and "first covenant" mentioned in verse 15 can- *Reasons for covenant.* not be properly rendered *testament*, but unquestionably refer back to vii, 22; viii, 6-10; and the same thought of *covenant* is continued in verse 18, where the first covenant is again referred to as having been

---
[1] It should be observed that every one of them is either a bare assertion or virtually a begging of the question at issue. The third and fifth of the assertions may be as truly affirmed of the view which insists on the sense of *covenant*.

144   THE MEDIATION OF JESUS CHRIST.

dedicated with blood.[1] (3) There is nothing, moreover, in the entire context to suggest the idea of a testamentary document, not even in the mention of "the eternal inheritance;" for that is conceived as a matter of God's *promise* (ἐπαγγελία), not as an estate bequeathed through forms of legal attestation. But covenants and promises are correlative ideas.[2] (4) A mediator of a covenant and a testator of a deed of bequest are not correlative ideas; so that to use the word in such a different meaning would be to introduce without justification an idea foreign to the Hebrew mind and unlikely to be employed in addressing Hebrews. (5) It may also be urged that the death of a testator is not necessary to make his will valid in law; no more so, at any rate, than the death of a covenant-maker is necessary to confirm a covenant. If it be strange and harsh to say that "where a covenant is, there must be of necessity the death of him that made it" (verse 16), is it not equally strange and very questionable as a matter of fact to say that a testament or will is valid only after the death of him that made it? In the case of the author, mediator, and finisher

---

[1] "The connection makes it most difficult to suppose that the key-word (διαθήκη) is used in different senses in the course of the verses, and especially that the characteristic of a particular kind of διαθήκη, essentially different from the *first covenant* of verses 15, 18, should be brought forward in verse 16. For it is impossible to maintain that the sacrifices with which the old covenant was inaugurated could be explained on the supposition that it was a *testament*. Nor does it appear that it could be called a *testament* in any sense."—Westcott, *The Epistle to the Hebrews*, p. 300. London, 1889.

[2] Compare the phrase "the covenants of the promise" in Eph. ii, 12, and compare Rom. ix, 4.

of our redemption from sin, such a statement about a testamentary deed has no relevancy, nor does it tend to illustrate any feature of the continuous mediatorial work of Christ. Any supposable word, testament, or declaration of the Christ must needs be as valid and sure before his death as after. (6) But the conspicuous fact of this new covenant is that the great mediator of it gave his own blood for the eternal redemption of those *who have been called* (οἱ κεκλημένοι), and the writer of this epistle makes this point most emphatic throughout the entire argument, and farther on he speaks of it as "the blood of the covenant," and "the blood of an eternal covenant" (x, 29; xiii, 20). (7) With this important fact in mind we should also observe that the *death,* which according to verse 15 "took place for the redemption of the transgressions that were under the first covenant," was the death of the mediator, Christ himself. (8) Accordingly, as stated above, the remarkable and unique feature of this new covenant is that its maker, mediator, and sacrificial victim, by whose blood the promise of the eternal inheritance is made forever fast and sure (βεβαία), are all one. This fact explains the boldness and apparent harshness of the language of verses 16 and 17, and it is in keeping with that style of thought which also conceives Christ as a throne of grace (iv, 16) and a mercy seat (Rom. iii, 25). (9) This interpretation, moreover, accords best with the words φέρεσθαι and ἐπὶ νεκροῖς in verses 16 and 17. If one would speak of *proving, attesting,* or *announcing* a

146   THE MEDIATION OF JESUS CHRIST.

person's *death*, he could not appropriately use the word φέρεσθαι, which might, indeed, refer to the *bringing forward* of a legal document for probate, but not to prove the *testator's death*. But the one manifestation of the Christ at the end of the ages for the putting away of sin by the sacrifice of himself (ix, 26) is fittingly designated by φέρεσθαι, which points to the bringing of his *death* forward into prominence,[1] and is equivalent to the *open setting forth* of Jesus Christ crucified, as in Gal. iii, 1, and the *setting him forth* as a mercy seat through faith in his blood, as in Rom. iii, 25. In this case the *death* of Christ, referred to in verse 15, is conceived as brought forward and set in strong light as the seal of the new covenant. The words ἐπὶ νεκροῖς, in verse 17, have peculiar force and significance in connection with the foregoing exposition, but are unsuitable for expressing the idea of the death of a testator. The phrase is seen in its true significance in connection with ratifying a covenant in Psa. l, 5, where ἐπὶ θυσίαις is employed by the Septuagint translators for the Hebrew עֲלֵי זָבַח, *over sacrifice:*

"Assemble unto me my pious ones,
Those that ratify my covenant *over sacrifice.*"[2]

---

[1] "It is not said that he who makes the covenant must die, but that his death must be *brought forward*, presented, introduced upon the scene, set in evidence, so to speak. This sense of φέρεσθαι appears to be perfectly natural, and to be more simple than the sense commonly attributed to the word, either to be alleged as a fact, or to be pleaded in the course of an argument, or to be current as a matter of common notoriety."—Westcott, *The Epistle to the Hebrews*, p. 265.

[2] The best illustration of the formalities of making or *cutting* a covenant (see the Hebrew Lexicons on the phrase כרת ברית)

COVENANT OVER DEAD VICTIMS. 147

To make or ratify a covenant it was necessary that a sacrificial victim or several victims be slain, and in the specific reference to the dedication of the first covenant which immediate- Covenants made over dead victims. ly follows in verses 18-22 Moses is mentioned as taking the blood of calves and goats and sprinkling it as the sign and seal of the covenant which God commanded (citing from Exod. xxiv, 8). Accordingly, the only suitable explanation of a covenant ἐπὶ νεκροῖς βεβαία would seem to be one *made strong over dead victims* slain for the purpose of ratifying the covenant. The death which "took place for the redemption of the transgressions" (verse 15), and also for providing "the blood of an everlasting covenant" (xiii, 20), is the death of Jesus Christ the mediator of the new covenant. This death, which marked a crisis of the ages, is brought forward into prominence, and is to furnish the solution of the apparent incongruity of making the mediator and sacrificial victim of the covenant one and the same. As high priest Jesus entered the holy places "through his own blood" (verse 12); as mediator and author and finisher of the new covenant he

---

over sacrifice is read in Gen. xv, 8-18, where Abram divides the dead victims, and places the parts over against each other, and the flaming torch is seen to pass between the pieces. The same custom of cutting and dividing the victims, and of passing between the portions is referred to in Jer. xxxiv, 18, 19. It will be noticed that the phrase ἐπὶ νεκροῖς, *over dead ones,* in Heb. ix, 17 (A. V., "after men are dead;" R. V., "where there hath been death") when used in reference to the ratification of a covenant, is virtually equivalent to ἐπὶ θυσίαις, *over sacrificial victims,* in Psa. l, 5. Compare also the phrases ἐπὶ βρώμασιν, πόμασιν, and βαπτισμοῖς, in Heb. ix, 10.

secures by his own death "the promise of the eternal inheritance" to all who have been called (verse 15); and so we are assured that the new covenant as truly as the first covenant has been consecrated with blood (verse 18), and it is as true under the one as under the other that "apart from the shedding of blood there is no remission" (verse 22). This significant symbolism of sacrifice and blood is prominent throughout the entire context (verses 13-22), and is not for a moment to be lost from view, or interrupted by a supposed irrelevant reference to the making and attesting of legal deeds of bequest.

With such an understanding of the main thoughts in this passage, it makes no essential difference whether we translate the last part of verse 17 affirmatively or interrogatively. The entire verse may be rendered thus: "For a covenant over dead (sacrificial victims) is firm, since it never has any force while the maker of it lives." That is, a covenant is confirmed on the basis and with the accompaniment of sacrifice, so that in reality it is without force or validity unless the covenant maker signify the surrender of his own life by the blood of the slain victims which he offers in the course of the solemn transaction.[1]

---

[1] Westcott has written so ably on this passage that we here add one more citation: "In ordinary covenants the death of the persons who made the covenant was represented of necessity in symbol only, and both parties were alike liable to change. . . . Here fresh considerations offer themselves which underlie the argument of the passage. The covenant to which the writer looks is not one between man and man, who meet as equal parties, but between man and God. The death of the covenant victim, therefore, assumes a new character. It figures not only the un-

NOT A COVENANT BETWEEN EQUALS. 149

In studying these illustrations which rest upon the customs and the symbolism of covenants, we must not overlook the fact that any covenant between God and man cannot be a covenant between equals. Such a covenant is, however, *This not a covenant between equals.* a most striking assurance of the gracious condescension of the Most High, and Jesus, as the mediator of the new covenant, represents in his redemptive work the interests of both God and man. These considerations serve to show also how, in the mind of the writer, covenant maker, mediator, and sacrificial offering all unite in the Son of God who is so remarkably described in the opening words of this epistle. This adorable mediator is heir of all things, maker of the ages, effulgence of the glory of God, upholder of all things, and purifier from all sin. Only such a transcendent Son of God can be at once maker, mediator, and sacrificial victim of an eternal covenant.

The foregoing study of Christ's priesthood and mediation as set forth in the Epistle to the Hebrews has doubtless put beyond question our statement that no other book of the New Testament furnishes so elaborate a discussion of this subject. *Uniqueness of the epistle.* The entire treatment is unique, and the learned critic and exegete cannot fail to note the Alexandrine cast of thought and the extensive and peculiar use of the Old Testament writings. These

---

changeableness of death, but also the self-surrender of death. . . . Christ was himself the covenant victim. In this aspect he attested the inviolable force of the covenant which he established."—*The Epistle to the Hebrews*, p. 302.

are recognized as a sacred deposit of heavenly truth; but the Septuagint version, not the Hebrew text, is uniformly quoted, and passages where this version differs notably from the Hebrew are made the basis of special argument and illustration.[1] The tabernacle and its holy places are looked upon as figures of heavenly realities opened to us through the mediation of Jesus Christ, and Melchizedek is extolled as a type of our high priest who is now seated at the right hand of the throne of God. But with all these and other peculiarities, which scientific exegesis must duly note, the teaching of this epistle on the subject of Christ's mediation is in fundamental harmony with the other books of the New Testament. The writer treats the death, exaltation, and everlasting intercession of our Lord much after the manner of Paul. Neither of these writers seems to know much of Jesus Christ in the days of his flesh, but they both magnify his heavenly exaltation. Paul emphasizes the idea of righteousness, and the writer to the Hebrews that of holiness; but so closely do they agree in the main that the Epistle to the Hebrews was long believed to be the work of

---

[1] Most notably so in x, 5, a citation of Psa. xl, 6, reads, "a *body* didst thou prepare for me," according to the Septuagint; but the Hebrew text of this passage reads, *"ears* thou hast dug for me," the word *dug* most naturally referring to the hollow cavity of the ear. However the error of the Greek version arose, the author of the epistle makes the word "body" significant by regarding it as the organ of Christ's incarnation and the means of *doing the will* of God. This is seen further in verse 10, where "the body of Jesus Christ" has obvious reference to this citation from the psalm. God "takes away the first," that is, sacrifices and offerings, "that he may establish the second," that is, the will of God.

Paul, and this opinion has not been without some advocates in quite recent times.[1] On the offering of the body and blood of Christ the teaching of the epistle is also remarkably like that of the First Epistle of Peter.

We find, then, that on the sacrifice and mediation of Christ all the New Testament writers are in substantial agreement. After showing due respect to the various classes of writings, and to their obvious individual peculiarities of thought and diction, we are compelled to acknowledge that according to all the Scriptures of the New Testament there is no salvation apart from Jesus Christ crucified, "nor is there any other name under heaven, that is given among men, wherein we must be saved." Peter and John and Paul and the author of Hebrews have their own ways of setting forth this truth, but none of them gets away from the doctrine which we trace in the words of Jesus at the last supper and at all those other times when he spoke of giving his life a ransom for many, or of laying it down in behalf of others.

Substantial agreement of all the New Testament writers.

---

[1] It is noteworthy that the English revisers of the New Testament so late as 1881 deemed it best to leave unchanged the title of "The Epistle of Paul the Apostle to the Hebrews."

CHAPTER XI.

CHRIST'S MEDIATION EFFICIENT THROUGH THE SPIRIT.

THE biblical doctrine of Christ's mediation cannot be fully presented without due recognition of the Holy Spirit working out the consummation of the purposed redemption. According to John's Gospel the departure

Departure of Christ expedient.
of Jesus from the world was expedient, and indeed necessary, for the highest good of the disciples and of those who should believe on Jesus through their word. "It is expedient for you that I go away: for if I go not away, the Comforter will not come unto you; but if I go, I will send him unto you" (John xvi, 7). The visible presence of Jesus Christ in the flesh was not compatible with the building of a universal Church of God and a household of faith possessed of the most exalted communion of saints. It was accordingly for the advantage of the disciples of Jesus, and for the consummation of the purposes of divine Love, that Jesus disappear from the gaze of the world. The spiritual and eternal things of God are not seen by mortal eyes (comp. 2 Cor. iv, 18), and the saving efficacy of the life and death and resurrection of the Lord Jesus has its perfect work through the mission and the ministries of the Holy Spirit.

THE COMFORTER. 153

It is only in the writings of John that the Holy Spirit is called THE COMFORTER (ὁ παράκλητος) (Gospel, xiv, 16, 26; xv, 26; xvi, 7; First Epistle, ii, 1). This word *Paraclete* may also be translated Helper, Advocate, Pleader, Intercessor, for all these ideas attach to the term as it is used; and one may well compare what Jesus says of the efficient advocacy and help of the Holy Spirit in the disciples when they are delivered up to the courts (Matt. x, 2; Mark xiii, 11). In 1 John ii, 1, "Jesus Christ the righteous" is himself called an "Advocate with the Father; that is, one who acts as intercessor and mediating high priest for us (comp. Heb. vii, 25; ix, 24; Rom. viii, 34). Being such an Advocate, he must needs also be our Helper and Comforter, and hence his own words in John xiv, 16-20, where our Lord implies that he is himself the Comforter, but will come to his disciples in the abiding presence of the Spirit of truth: "I will pray the Father, and he shall give you another Comforter (such as I am now), that he may abide with you forever, even the Spirit of truth: whom the world cannot receive; for it beholdeth him not, neither knoweth him: ye know him; for he abideth with you and shall be in you. I will not leave you desolate (like orphans): I will come unto you. Yet a little while and the world beholdeth me no more; but ye behold me: because I live, ye shall live also. In that day ye shall know that I am in my Father, and ye in me, and I in you."

The Comforter.

It is to be observed that this heavenly Comforter is

sent or given by the Father at the prayer and in the name of Jesus (xiv, 16, 26); he "proceedeth from

Procession and personality of the Spirit. ($\dot{\epsilon}\kappa\pi o\rho\epsilon\acute{v}\epsilon\tau\alpha\iota$, *goeth forth from*) the Father" (xv, 26), and bears witness of Christ. He is to take the place of Jesus with the disciples, and so Jesus himself declares, "I will send him unto you from the Father." We need not wonder, then, that in 2 Cor. iii, 17, 18, the Lord Christ is himself called the Spirit, and in other epistles "the Spirit of God" and "the Spirit of Christ" are interchangeable terms. So in the mystic and mysterious relations of Father, Son, and Holy Spirit we are to recognize an adorable Unity. The Son is the only begotten of the Father; the Spirit proceedeth from the Father; the Son and the Spirit are alike sent by the Father, and the Spirit is sent both by the Father and the Son. These truths become still more impressive when we compare the trinitarian formula in 2 Cor. xiii, 14: "The grace of the Lord Jesus Christ, and the love of God, and the communion of the Holy Spirit." The same distinction appears in the baptismal formula of Matt. xxviii, 19: "The name of the Father, and of the Son, and of the Holy Spirit." A like distinction is seen in the salutation of Rev. i, 4, 5: "Grace and peace (1) from him who is and who was and who is to come, and (2) from the seven Spirits before his throne, and (3) from Jesus Christ." In the foregoing examples we note that Jesus Christ, or the Son, holds the first place in the first text, the second place in the second text, and the third place in Rev. i, 5. We also find that each of

THE SPIRIT OF GOD. 155

these hallowed names is again and again mentioned in the New Testament as the source and means of divine help, and yet at times the Father is spoken of as distinctively the source *from whom* (ἐξ οὗ), and the Son as the one *through whom* (διὰ οὗ), and the Holy Spirit as the one *in whom* (ἐν ᾧ), or by whose efficient agency, all things are.[1]

The Scriptures furnish us no definition of the word *spirit*. The Hebrew רוּחַ and the Greek πνεῦμα have the same meaning, usage, and connotation as the Latin *spiritus*, which has become familiarly Anglicized, and is employed in the same variety of signification, namely, breath, wind, courage, disposition, temper, vital principle which animates all sentient life. In its highest sense it designates that rational element in man to which we attribute feeling, thinking, and volition, and the word may be applied to God in the same general way. "The spirit of a man," however, is a phrase that commonly distinguishes his higher rational nature from his bodily form, while the phrase "Spirit of God" points rather to the essential quality of his nature. "God is Spirit" (John iv, 24). Spirit constitutes, so to speak, the characteristic element and totality of his nature. But in the Eternal Spirit we assume the same trinal con-

The Spirit of God.

---

[1] See 1 Cor. viii, 6; xi, 12; xii, 3; Rom. vi, 23; xv, 16; xvi, 27; 1 Thess. i, 5. "In every work," says Kuyper, "effected by Father, Son, and Holy Ghost in common, the power *to bring forth* proceeds from the Father; the power *to arrange*, from the Son; the power *to perfect*, from the Holy Spirit."—*The Work of the Holy Spirit*, p. 19. New York, 1900.

stituents of personality as in the spirit of man—will, feeling, and intelligence. Man exists in the image and glory of God (Gen. i, 26; 1 Cor. xi, 7), and in Christ "dwelleth all the fullness of the Godhead bodily" (Col. ii, 9). These two important truths may enable us to see more clearly how "God was in Christ reconciling the world unto himself." Conceived as the Logos or Word of God, Christ is the wisdom of God, the thought, reason, intelligence of the divine Personality, and in his incarnation he reveals at once the glory of heavenly wisdom, love, and power. But as all the fullness of Deity found bodily expression *through him,* and yet he was distinctively the Word, so in the Father dwelleth all the fullness of the Godhead potentially and actively, and all things are accordingly *from him;* while in the Holy Spirit dwelleth all the fullness of the Godhead efficiently. And so all the fullness of God becomes operative and personally present in the world and in the spirit of man by the power of the Holy Spirit. Thus the Lord Christ and the Father dwell personally and lovingly in him who loves Christ and keeps his word: "My Father will love him, and WE will come unto him, and make our abode with him" (John xiv, 23).

Whatever mysterious distinctions exist in the personal nature of the Godhead, we must according to John's Gospel recognize the Holy Spirit, the Comforter,

<small>The Spirit one with God.</small> as essentially one with God. If in the deepest sense God is spirit, the Spirit of God and God himself are one. We are, therefore,

PERSONALITY OF THE SPIRIT. 157

not to think of this eternal Spirit as merely an influence, an energy, or some impersonal emanation flowing out from God, but as the personal God himself, the creative, sustaining, ever-present Spirit. The Spirit of God is described in Gen. i, 2, as "brooding over the face of the waters," and acting as the all-powerful Generatrix of swarms of living things which come forth from the waters by the Word of God (comp. verse 20). The Hebrew poets conceive the heavens as made and garnished by the Spirit as truly as by the Word of God (Psa. xxxiii, 6; civ, 30; Job xxvi, 13; xxxiii, 4). In the parallelism of Psa. cxxxix, 7, the Spirit of Jehovah and his presence are conceived as ubiquitous:

> "Whither shall I go from thy Spirit?
> Or whither shall I flee from thy presence?"

The prophets also represent or assume that the Spirit of Jehovah is the same as Jehovah himself (comp. Isa. xl, 13; xlviii, 16; lxi, 1; lxiii, 10; Ezek. xi, 5; Zech. iv, 6; vii, 12).

It is also worthy of notice that in John's Gospel, the personality of the Spirit, the Comforter, is made peculiarly emphatic by means of the masculine form of the pronoun. Not only have we the masculine ὁ παράκλητος, *the Comforter,* but the demonstrative ἐκεῖνος is repeatedly employed in referring to the Spirit. The Greek word πνεῦμα is a neuter noun, and any pronoun coming in immediate connection should grammatically take the neuter form. Hence such examples as the following are noteworthy: "The Comforter, the Holy Spirit, . . . he (ἐκεῖνος) shall teach you all things" (John xiv, 26). The same construction appears again in xv, 26, and xvi, 13, 14. In the last-named passage the use of ἐκεῖνος is the more striking, since it is used in immediate appositive connection with τό πνεῦμα τῆς ἀληθείας, *the Spirit of truth.* Such a remarkable use of the personal pronoun is not fairly explained by way of personification, for the personal acts of God himself are conspicuously set forth.[1]

From what we have now observed touching the nature and operation of the Holy Spirit, three things may be affirmed: (1) God is essentially Spirit, and the Spirit of God is no other than the Holy One himself; but what is written about the Spirit "proceeding from the Father," and the sending of the Spirit by the Father and the Son, the pouring out of the Spirit, as on the day of Pentecost, and other like expressions concerning the power and gifts of the Spirit, lead us to think of the Holy Spirit as in some specific sense a manifestation of the active sympathy of God with man, and of his personal coöperation with those children of God who delight to

Three fundamental truths.

---

[1] "The Spirit here spoken of is a personal existence. Personal epithets are applied to him, and the actions ascribed to him are personal actions. He is to be the substitute of the most marked and influential Personality with whom the disciples had ever been brought into contact. He is to supply his vacated place. He is to be to the disciples as friendly and stanch an ally and a more constantly present and efficient teacher than Christ himself."—Marcus Dods, in *Expositor's Bible*, Gospel of John, *in loco*.

PROMISE OF THE FATHER.   159

do his will. In order that the divers operations of the
Spirit might accomplish their perfect work, it (2) was
necessary for Jesus to appear among men, proclaim
the coming of the kingdom of God, and give his life a
ransom for man. It was expedient and necessary that
he should go away from the gaze of men, and with his
Father send the Comforter in his place to be the efficient executive of the Godhead in the salvation of men
and the regeneration of the world. (3) The signal
event of the outpouring of the Spirit at Pentecost was
a specific fulfillment of Jesus's promise of the Comforter, and it is called, in Acts i, 4, "the promise of the
Father." That event indicated the near approach of a
new age, "the age to come," of which the prophets and
the Christ had spoken, a dispensation of the Spirit.
From that time onward men were to learn that the
heavenly excellence, and the "eternal life, which was
with the Father and was manifested" in Christ, must
be realized through faith in the unseen, and not by
fleshly sight. All these facts and truths have vital
connection with the redeeming ministry of our Lord
Jesus Christ, and cannot be separated from a full
biblical conception of his priestly mediation.[1]

In the light of these truths we see that the saving
mediation of Jesus Christ is now no finished work, but

---

[1] "The Spirit of the Incarnate," says R. C. Moberly, "is the
Spirit of God. But it is not so much the Spirit of God, regarded
in his eternal existence, or relation, in the being of Deity; it is
the Spirit of God in humanity, the Spirit of God become the
Spirit of man in the person of the Incarnate—it is this which is
the distinctive significance and life of the Church of Christ."—
Atonement and Personality, p. 195. New York, 1901.

a process of salvation going on in the manifold operations of the Comforter, the Spirit of
truth. To use the figure of Heb. vii, 25,
and ix, 24, Christ has entered into the heavenly holy
of holies, and now appears before the face of God for
us, ever living to make intercession for the many sons
whom he brings into glory. It accords beautifully
with these conceptions of Christly mediation that we
find in the beginning of John's Apocalypse (i, 4) an
invocation of grace and peace "from the seven Spirits
which are before the throne." We
note the mention of these "seven
Spirits" between the threefold designation of the
Eternal, who is and was and is to come, and Jesus
Christ who "loosed us from our sins in his blood." It
appears farther on that "the Living One," who was
dead but is alive for the ages of ages and holds the
keys of death, also holds in his right hand "the seven
stars which are the angels of the seven churches." He
is furthermore said to hold or "have the seven Spirits
of God" (iii, 1). The apocalyptist also saw "seven
lamps of fire burning before the throne, which are the
seven Spirits of God" (iv, 5), and in a later vision
he beheld "in the midst of the throne a Lamb standing
as though it had been slain, having seven eyes, which
are the seven Spirits of God, sent forth into all the
earth" (v, 6). This language reminds us of Zech-
ariah's vision of "seven eyes of Jehovah that run to
and fro through the whole earth" (Zech. iii, 9; iv, 10),
and language and symbols are characteristic of apoca-

lyptic writings. "The seven Spirits that are before the throne" of the Eternal are no other than the Holy Spirit, the Comforter that proceedeth from the Father, and cooperates with Father and Son in effecting the redemption of mankind. The mystical significance of the number seven, as here referring to the Holy Spirit, in all probability prompted the ancient Christian hymn:

> "Thou the anointing Spirit art,
> Who dost thy sevenfold gifts impart."

These sevenfold gifts may, perhaps, be fairly represented in those diverse operations of the Spirit which are commonly designated by the terms "conviction," "regeneration," "bearing witness with our spirit," "sanctifying," "revealing the truth," "anointing with power," and "comforting." It is not important that we assign these manifold works of the Spirit to just seven forms of gracious help. These may be more or fewer, as various experiences show, but the seven well-known works of the Spirit named above are sufficiently comprehensive for our purpose in pointing out the continuous mediation of Christ through the Holy Spirit. *[margin: Seven operations of the Spirit.]*

1. *Conviction.* According to what we read in John xvi, 8, it is one leading purpose of the Comforter to "convict the world in respect of sin, and of righteousness, and of judgment." The word here rendered *convict* ($\dot{\epsilon}\lambda\acute{\epsilon}\gamma\chi\omega$) carries with it the idea of exposing things in their true light. It involves the process and the result of a searching test which is sure to bring

condemnation, reproof, and shame to the evildoer. "All things when they are *reproved* (ἐλεγχόμενα) are made manifest by the light" (Eph. v, 13). And so it is said in John iii, 20, that the evildoer hates the light and refuses to come to the light lest his works should be reproved (ἐλεγχϑῇ, *exposed to severe censure* and the shame of open conviction). But according to Jesus the conviction effected by the Spirit of truth has regard to sin, righteousness, and judgment in a manner which he goes on to indicate in verses 9-11: "Of sin, because they believe not on me; of righteousness, because I go to the Father, and ye behold me no more; of judgment, because the prince of this world has been judged." The meaning of these words is not apparent at first sight, for it involves a depth and scope of religious conception peculiar to the most profound sayings of the Fourth Gospel. The Lord Jesus is speaking from his own elevated point of view, and seems to contemplate the whole period and work of the Spirit's operations in one comprehensive glance. As the devil once "showed him all the kingdoms of the world in a moment of time" (Luke iv, 5), so now the eternal Spirit opens in one moment the vision of all the ages to his eye. The language implies a crucial hour like that of chapter xii, 31, 32: "Now is the judgment of this world: now shall the prince of this world be cast out. And I, if I be lifted up from the earth, will draw all men unto myself." The words should therefore be interpreted as a momentary eonic conception of the world (κόσμος).

SIN, RIGHTEOUSNESS, AND JUDGMENT. 163

There are three things concerning which the Spirit works conviction, namely, sin, righteousness, and judgment. The world is convicted περὶ ἁμαρτίας, *"concerning sin,* because they believe not on me." (Conviction concerning sin.) As in the judgment picture of Matt. xxv, 31-46, all sin and all righteousness of the persons judged were determined by the relations and activities of those persons toward the Son of man, who there appears upon his judgment throne, so here all sin is viewed as a failure or a refusal to believe on Christ. Being the Light of the world, he becomes the supreme test of all human hearts in their relation to truth; for "this is the condemning judgment, that the light is come into the world" (iii, 19). And therefore Jesus says: "If I had not come and spoken unto them, they had not had sin: but now they have no excuse for their sin" (xv, 22; comp. Acts xvii, 30, 31). Christ is the supreme revelation of God, and the most fearful and fatal form of sin is a persistent and blasphemous rejection of the truth when it comes with the clearest conviction of the Spirit to one's heart. And so all sin is shown, in its real nature, by persistent refusal of the manifested truth of God. We need not say that all sin consists in unbelief of Christ, but rather that he is the typical sinner, whose attitude toward Christ as "the way, and the truth, and the life" (xiv, 6) is that of persistent unbelief. It is in the light of this sort of conviction concerning sin that John writes: "Who is the liar but he who denies that Jesus is the Christ? This is the antichrist—he who denies the Father and the Son" (1 John ii, 22). The Spirit of truth that proceeds from the Father, and witnesses of Christ, is the living agent who convinces the sinful heart of its personal guilt by disclosing what sin is. It is by the direct working of this Spirit that the word of God becomes "living, and active, and sharper than any two-edged sword, and piercing even to the dividing of soul and spirit, of both joints and marrow, and quick to discern the thoughts and intents of the heart" (Heb. iv, 12).

But the convincing power of the Spirit deals also with *righteousness*, the direct contrast and opposite of sin. And as sin has its seat and manifestation in the heart of the unbelieving world, so, on the other hand, righteousness has found its supreme exhibition in Him who could calmly say before his enemies, "Who among you convicteth me of sin?" (viii, 46.) The spotless righteousness of Christ is the most conspicuous possible antithesis of the sin of the world, and his going unto the Father so that his disciples behold him no more in the flesh has exalted, completed, and glorified this ideal of righteousness into absolute perfection. He was and shall forever be "the righteous one" (Acts iii, 14; vii, 52; xxii, 14; 1 Pet. iii, 18; 1 John ii, 1; James v, 6). He is the only being who could pray: "O righteous Father, the world knew thee not, but I knew thee; and these knew that thou didst send me; and I make known unto them thy name, and will make it known" (John xvii, 25, 26). It was expedient for him to go

SIN, RIGHTEOUSNESS, AND JUDGMENT. 165

unto the Father, and being thus glorified, to send forth the living Spirit of truth, convince the world concerning righteousness, and make this perfect ideal of righteousness forever monumental. It was also expedient for him to go away from the gaze of his disciples in order that they thenceforth might live by faith, not by sight, and that the righteousness of faith might become the blessed possession of every believer (comp. Rom. iii, 21, 22).

Furthermore, the Spirit is to convict the world *"concerning judgment,* because the prince of this world has been judged." Twice before in this Gospel has "the prince of this world" been mentioned (xii, 31; xiv, 30), and he is no doubt to be identified with the devil, of whom it is said, in viii, 44, that "he was a murderer from the beginning, and stands not in the truth, because there is no truth in him." He is the arch-antichrist, and hath nothing in common with the Son of God (comp. xiv, 30). The prince of light stands in essential opposition to the prince of darkness, and according to 1 John iii, 8, "The Son of God was manifested that he might destroy the works of the devil." Therefore the eternal Spirit of truth, who witnesses of Christ and reveals the things of God, must needs pass condemning judgment on the enemy of all righteousness. This judgment of the prince of this world, as expressed here and in xii, 31, covers the whole period of the dispensation of the Spirit, and yet seems like the vision of a moment, as when Jesus "beheld Satan fallen as lightning from heaven" (Luke x, 18). It is in truth a process extending through all the centuries required for drawing all men unto Christ.[1] It is a judgment that exposes the wiles of the devil, exhibits him as the bitter enemy of all truth, and declares what his penal sentence has been and must ever be. Hence the force of the perfect in the verb κέκριται, *has been judged;* is already adjudged to condemnation. And such judgment of the prince of this world is also the condemnation which the Spirit of truth must needs pronounce against all workers of iniquity who, Satan-like, oppose and exalt themselves against God. And so, in the parable of eternal judgment in Matt. xxv, 31-46, the Son of man, sitting on the throne of his glory, executes this judgment of the Spirit when he says to those on his left hand, "Depart from me, ye cursed, into the eternal fire, which is prepared for the devil and his angels." Thus, in every case, the work of conviction concerning sin, righteousness, and judgment, brings out into unmistakable certainty the real nature of both the evil and the good.

2. *Regeneration.* That mighty work of the Holy Spirit of God whereby one is "delivered out of the power of darkness and translated into the kingdom of the Son of his love" (Col. i, 13; comp. 1 Pet. ii, 9) is

---

[1] "That which was to be effected by his Spirit in the Church during the whole course of ages down to the end of the world, he concentrates, as it were, into a single point of space, and a single moment of time; even as our eye, with the help of distance, concentrates a world into a star."—Hare, *The Mission of the Comforter,* p. 38. London, 1876.

spoken of in John iii, 5-8, as being "born of the Spirit." Whosoever is thus begotten of God is conceived as a "new creation" (2 Cor. v, 17; Gal. vi, 15), "created in Christ Jesus for good works" (Eph. ii, 10), "the new man, who after God hath been created in righteousness and holiness of truth" (Eph. iv, 24). This mighty change is also conceived a being raised from the dead so as to "walk in newness of life" (Rom. vi, 4), and even the quickening of our mortal bodies into the resurrection life is through the power of the indwelling Spirit (Rom. viii, 11). The new birth, conceived as a new creation and a resurrection from a state of death, is thus enhanced in our thought as essentially a supernatural work wrought within us, but it is effected by the specific agency of the Spirit of God. And so it is written, "According to his mercy he saved us, through the washing of regeneration and renewing of the Holy Spirit" (Titus iii, 5).

3. *Sanctification.* Regeneration, strictly speaking, only introduces one into newness of spiritual life. "The law of the Spirit of life in Christ Jesus" makes and keeps one free from the law of sin and of death (Rom. viii, 2). He that is dead unto sin cannot live any longer therein (Rom. vi, 2). "Whosoever doeth not righteousness is not of God," and "hereby we know that we abide in him, and he in us, because he hath given us of his Spirit" (1 John iii, 10; iv, 13). All growth in the Christian life, and all deepening and perfecting of Christian graces, come through the continual supply and ministration of the Spirit (Phil.

168   THE MEDIATION OF JESUS CHRIST.

i, 19; Gal. iii, 5). So we read of the "sanctification of the Spirit" (1 Pet. i, 2; 2 Thess. ii, 13; comp. Rom. xv, 16). All the saints of God "are sanctified in Christ Jesus" (1 Cor. i, 2), but the sanctification like the washing of regeneration, and justification in the name of Christ, is effected and realized "in the Spirit of our God" (1 Cor. vi, 11). The Holy Spirit operates directly in the human spirit by means of every instrument of truth, and Jesus prayed that the disciples might be sanctified in the truth (John xvii, 17). We noticed above that the Spirit's work of conviction was wrought through the word of divine revelation, which discerns the thoughts and intents of the heart (Heb. iv, 12); sanctification of the heart is effected by the same mighty instrument of truth. "The Spirit of truth" must needs appropriate and employ the truth in the entire sanctification of one's spirit and soul and body (1 Thess. v, 23).

He who truly walks in newness of life lives by the Spirit and walks by the Spirit (Gal. v, 25). The purified soul that is blessed with the vision of God is "transformed into the same image from glory to glory by the Lord, the Spirit" (2 Cor. iii, 18). Here the Lord Jesus Christ is himself called the Spirit (verse 17), and those who are transformed into his image [1]

---

[1] Mahan observes: "The Spirit sanctifies by presenting Christ to the mind in such a manner that we are transformed into his image. The common error of Christians, in respect to this subject, seems to be this—looking away from Christ to the Holy Spirit for sanctification, instead of looking for the Spirit to render Christ their sanctification."—*Christian Perfection*, p. 172.

WITNESS OF THE SPIRIT. 169

are also spoken of as "epistles of Christ, written with the Spirit of the living God" (verse 3). The abiding presence of the Spirit is a personal fellowship or communion (2 Cor. xiii, 14; Phil. ii, 1) which promotes sanctification of the human spirit, and the love of God is shed abroad in the heart by the Holy Spirit (Rom. v, 5). "Joy in the Holy Spirit" (Rom. xiv, 17) is a phrase worthy of notice in the same connection, for fellowship, love, and joy point to high and blessed attainments of the sanctified. "The earnest of the Spirit" (2 Cor. i, 22; v, 5), which is given the believer as both a foretaste and a pledge of his inheritance in God's own possession (Eph. i, 14), is an expression which richly enhances the holy fellowship of God, and being "sealed with the Holy Spirit of promise" (Eph. i, 13; iv, 30) adds to the thought of foretaste and pledge the idea of God's fixing thereon the special stamp of his personal assurance. The privilege of being "filled with the Spirit" (Eph. v, 18; Acts ix, 17; xi, 24) is also a good assurance that the pentecostal baptism of the Spirit (comp. Acts ii, 4) is available unto all who will receive it. By these manifold attainments of holy life in the Spirit one "comes to know the love of Christ which passeth knowledge," and apprehends how he "may be filled unto all the fullness of God" (Eph. iii, 19).

4. *Witness and Communion.* Another specific work of the Holy Spirit is to impart directly to each child of God the assuring testimony that he is born from above. The classic text is Rom. viii, 16: "The Spirit

himself beareth witness with our spirit, that we are children of God." This divine assurance is also necessarily involved in the establishing and anointing, referred to in 2 Cor. i, 21, 22, as a work of God, "who also sealed us and gave us the earnest of the Spirit in our hearts." Paul speaks in Rom. ix, 1, of his own conscience bearing witness with him in the Spirit. John says (1 John v, 7) that "it is the Spirit that beareth witness, because the Spirit is the truth." "Hereby we know that he abideth in us, by the Spirit that he gave us" (1 John iii, 24). This witness of the Spirit is the assuring conviction of the new birth and of the spiritual life which is wrought in the heart by the direct agency of the Holy Spirit of God. The abiding presence or "communion (κοινωνία, *fellowship*, 2 Cor. xiii, 14; Phil. ii, 1) of the Holy Spirit" must needs be of essentially the same nature, an assuring continual conviction that our new life in the Spirit "is hid with Christ in God" (Col. iii, 3). Our filial relation to God is thus impressed upon us as a blessed conviction, and so long as that conviction remains we cry, Abba, Father, thereby witnessing on our part that we are children of God.

5. *Revealing the Truth.* Along with this assuring witness of the Spirit we should also notice the direct agency of the same Spirit in communicating light and knowledge and wisdom to the soul. He is called emphatically "the Spirit of truth," and comes to "guide into all the truth," to take of the things of Christ and declare them to the heart and conscience of the believer

REVEALING THE TRUTH.   171

(John xvi, 13-15). In this passage the Spirit is spoken of as *hearing* the things he makes known, just as in xv, 15, Jesus says, "All things that I heard from my Father I have made known unto you." The Son and the Spirit hear of God the things they reveal: they are alike partakers of those divine secrets which it has pleased the heavenly Father to reveal unto men. But the Spirit declares the things of Christ and so continues his ministry of heavenly revelation. It is this Spirit of truth who enables us "to know the mysteries of the kingdom of heaven" (comp. Matt. xiii, 11, and xi, 25). Thus the Holy Spirit bears witness of Christ (John xv, 26). All this accords most closely with what is written in 1 Cor. ii, 9-14: "Things which eye saw not, and ear heard not, and which entered not into the heart of man, whatsoever things God prepared for them that love him, (these things) God revealed unto us through the Spirit." These are called "the things of the Spirit of God," which the natural man cannot receive or know. This communicating of truth by the Spirit is called in 1 John ii, 20, 27, "an anointing from the Holy One." "The anointing which ye received of him abideth in you, and ye need not that anyone teach you; but his anointing teacheth you concerning all things, and is true." This Spirit also reveals the future and "declares the things that are to come" (John xvi, 13), and also brings to mind the sayings of Jesus (xiv, 26). These operations of the Spirit show that he is the great Illuminator, who flashes light upon the human understanding, so that in his light we see light

(Psa. xxxvi, 9). So the psalmists and prophets were in some sense organs of the Spirit (comp. Heb. iii, 7; Matt. xxii, 43; 2 Sam. xxiii, 2), when they uttered the oracles of God. "Men spoke from God, being moved by the Holy Spirit" (2 Pet. i, 21; comp. 1 Pet. i, 11). The Holy Scriptures were thus God-breathed (2 Tim. iii, 16), and hence their profitableness for teaching and instruction in righteousness. For thus one becomes "filled with the knowledge of God's will in all spiritual wisdom and understanding" (Col. i, 9; comp. Eph. i, 17, 18). The sons of God are led by the Spirit of God (Rom. viii, 14; Gal. v, 18). And we should not overlook the fact that the Messianic Branch to come forth from the stock of Jesse was to be gifted with the Spirit of wisdom and understanding, the Spirit of counsel, and the Spirit of knowledge (Isa. xi, 2). It is also profoundly suggestive in the symbolism of Rev. v, 5, 6, that the Root of David appears as a Lamb "having seven eyes, which are the seven Spirits of God, sent forth into all the earth." He thus represents "the wisdom of God."

6. *Imparting Gifts of Power.* The Spirit of Jehovah which was to rest upon the Branch of Jesse, according to the prophecy of Isa. xi, 2, was to be also a "Spirit of power," and Jesus bade the disciples tarry in Jerusalem "until clothed with power from on high" (Luke xxiv, 49). "Ye shall receive power," he said (Acts i, 8), "when the Holy Spirit is come upon you." The great outpouring of the Spirit which came upon the disciples at Pentecost was the first signal fulfill-

GIFTS OF THE SPIRIT. 173

ment of that "promise of the Father;" but the same blessed gift is an abiding power in the Church of God. Jesus went to the Father and was seen no more; but the Spirit was sent as his invisible Executive to abide permanently. "He abideth (μένει) with you and shall be in you" (John xiv, 17). Paul speaks of "the power of the Holy Spirit" (Rom. xv, 13, 19), and of "being made powerful in all power according to the might of his glory" (Col. i, 11), and "being strengthened with power through his Spirit in the inward man" (Eph. iii, 16). After his temptation Jesus "returned in the power of the Spirit into Galilee" (Luke iv, 14), and every disciple who has since that time triumphed over evil has done so in the power of the same Holy Spirit. "It is the Spirit that giveth life" (John vi, 63; 2 Cor. iii, 6), and "the last Adam, the man from heaven, is a life-giving Spirit" (1 Cor. xv, 45); and so the power of God which effects the resurrection of the dead (comp. Matt. xxii, 29; 1 Cor. vi, 14) is exerted and becomes effective through the Spirit (Rom. viii, 11, 23). As the first awakening of the soul of man from the death of sin and his regeneration into newness of life is accomplished by the power of the Holy Spirit, so the uttermost consummation of his redemption is to be realized by means of the mighty working of the same Spirit. And all this is "according to the working (ἐνέργεια) whereby the Lord Jesus Christ is able to subject all things unto himself" (Phil. iii, 21). Thus we see that the phrase "the power of the Holy Spirit" (Rom. xv, 13, 19) is essentially equivalent to the power of God. The apostle speaks of preaching the gospel "in demonstration of the Spirit and of power" (1 Cor. ii, 4; comp. 1 Thess. i, 5; 2 Cor. vi, 6, 7), and all human efficiency in the ministries of the gospel and the propagation of the truth of God in the world must needs be through the power of the Holy Spirit, which is the only real "power from on high."

Among the Spirit's gifts of power we also note those extraordinary charisms of the early Church which are referred to in Heb. ii, 4: "God bearing witness both by signs and wonders, and by manifold powers and distributions of the Holy Spirit, according to his will." These remarkable manifestations are thus described in 1 Cor. xii, 4-11: "Now there are diversities of gifts, but the same Spirit. . . . To each one is given the manifestation of the Spirit to profit withal. For to one is given through the Spirit the word of wisdom; and to another the word of knowledge, according to the same Spirit: to another faith, in the same Spirit; and to another gifts of healings, in the one Spirit; and to another workings of powers ($\delta\upsilon\nu\acute{\alpha}\mu\epsilon\omega\nu$, *of miracles*); and to another prophecy; and to another discernings of spirits: to another kinds of tongues; and to another the interpretation of tongues: but all these worketh the one and the same Spirit, dividing to each one severally even as he will."[1] These manifold gifts of

Gifts of the Spirit.

---

[1] Whedon classifies these divers charisms "into gifts of *mind*, of *voice*, and of *action*; thought, word, and deed. Under mind are gifts of wisdom, knowledge, faith, discerning of spirits, and interpretation; under gifts of voice or utterance, prophecy and

THE COMFORTER.	175

power have been distributed into great diversities of ministrations, manifesting themselves at certain times and places more notably than at others. But altogether they give assurance of the mighty energy with which the Holy Spirit ever worketh to consummate the age-long triumphs of the kingdom of God and of Christ.

7. *The Comforter.* Finally, if in the foregoing outline we have omitted any distinctive form or quality of the manifold operations of the Spirit, all that remains to be noticed may be comprehended under the word *Paraclete* (παράκλητος), which our English versions of the New Testament have commonly translated *Comforter.* The word is found only in the writings of John (xiv, 16, 26; xv, 26; xvi, 7; 1 John ii, 1), and we have already observed that, in the one passage in the First Epistle where it occurs, it is explicitly applied to Jesus Christ as our "Advocate with the Father." And when Jesus says, in John xiv, 16, that the Father "will give you another Paraclete" he clearly implies that the title is also truly descriptive of himself. It is generally admitted that *Comforter* is not an adequate translation of παράκλητος; the primary meaning of the Greek word is that of *advocate,* as commonly rendered in 1 John ii, 1. It designates one who pleads the cause of another, and acts as his legal counselor and friend. The Paraclete is a helper, an official friend at court, an advocate, who not only keeps himself in closest touch with those who desire his assistance, but is also

---

tongues; under gifts of action, healing and working of miracles."
—*Commentary on the New Testament, in loco.*

ever ready to plead their cause in time of need. And so "the Spirit helpeth our infirmity," and "maketh intercession for the saints according to God" (Rom. viii, 26, 27). Such a divine helper in our times of need is a great Comforter, and hence the propriety of this title to represent the Spirit of truth as an abiding Helper. There is unspeakable comfort in the promise that "he may be with you forever;" "he abideth with you, and shall be in you" (John xiv, 17). Moreover, the Greek words παρακαλέω and παράκλησις are not infrequently used in the sense of bringing comfort and consolation. "The God and Father of our Lord Jesus Christ, the Father of mercies," is called "the God of all comfort, who comforteth us in all our affliction, that we may be able to comfort them that are in any affliction, through the comfort wherewith we ourselves are comforted of God" (2 Cor. i, 3, 4). In Acts ix, 31, we read of "the comfort of the Holy Spirit."

Such, according to the Scriptures, are the sevenfold manifestations of the Spirit, and these divers ministrations of the personal "Power from on high" are the source of all life and growth in the kingdom of God. Through the continuous and unfailing work of the Holy Spirit of truth the kingdom of heaven cometh, and the will of God is done on earth as in heaven. And in all these ways our Lord continues his saving mediation, and "God is in Christ reconciling the world unto himself."

CHAPTER XII.

SUMMARY OF THE BIBLICAL DOCTRINE.

HAVING now examined with some care the import of the language of the biblical writers touching the mediation of Jesus Christ, we shall conclude this essay with a brief statement of the principal truths which may be read in these scriptures and clearly proved thereby. Our statements in this epitome of doctrine are of the nature of so many expressions of conviction as to the real teaching of the various portions of Scripture which we have examined and endeavored to expound, and they should, accordingly, be read as the results of a faithful exegetical study of the word of truth rather than as the dogmas of a formulated creed.

Results of exegesis.

1. Our first observation is that the mediatorial ministry of Jesus Christ is a continuous process, not a finished work. We are not authorized by any biblical teaching to maintain that such terms as atonement, propitiation, expiation, and redemption, as applied to the saving ministry of our Lord, imply that he has completed or is near the completion of the work for which he came into the world. He truly died, and thus offered himself "once for all" (Rom. vi, 10; Heb. vii, 27; ix, 12, 26, 28; x, 10; 1 Pet. iii, 18); that fact is

A continuous process, not a finished work.

simple and definite matter of history; but that particular event was, relatively, only an incident in the vast work of Christ's mediation. It was only the passing of our great high priest into the heavenly holy of holies "through his own blood," that he might appear in the presence of God for us, and there abide forever as our high priest and mediator. How could his being "delivered up for our trespasses" have availed had he not also been "raised for our justification"? (Rom. iv, 25.) According to Paul, "It is Christ Jesus that died, yea rather, that was raised from the dead, who is at the right hand of God, who also maketh intercession for us" (Rom. viii, 34). And according to this apostle it is also the Holy Spirit that "maketh intercession for the saints according to the will of God" (Rom. viii, 27), and in 2 Cor. iii, 17, he calls our Lord himself the Spirit who transforms us into the image of the glory of God. The eternal Spirit and Christ and God are one in all this ministry of reconciliation, and the Lord Christ has no more finished his work of mediation than has the Holy Father or the Holy Spirit finished yearning for mankind. The heavenly redemption is thus seen to be a process that must needs go on so long as there remains one sinner to be saved.

2. The nature of Christ's mediation is largely set forth by means of metaphors and symbols. This fact should admonish us that greatest care must be exercised in our interpretations of biblical texts bearing on this

Largely set forth by symbols and metaphors.

METAPHORICAL LANGUAGE. 179

subject.¹ Human language is at best imperfect, and there are some figures of speech from which, perhaps, no two men would derive precisely the same idea. We need not wonder, therefore, that divers theories of atonement have sought support in what on close analysis appears to be only incidental features of an object referred to in a metaphor. We have seen that the New Testament writers speak often of the saving work of Christ in terms that plainly derive their significance from the sacrificial ceremonies of the Jewish people, and their language cannot be fairly interpreted without attention to Old Testament facts and teachings concerning the offering of blood upon the altar. Such words as *atonement, propitiation,* and *expiation*² are

---

¹ Due regard must also be had for peculiar forms of expression which characterize particular writers. There are mystical sayings which are peculiarly Johannine, and for that very reason not to be understood as if they were of the nature of a dogmatic formula. There are also texts and paragraphs in Paul's writings which evince his rabbinical training, and also bold realistic statements which may by valid exegesis be resolved into mystical or ideal conceptions. It is a misleading procedure for anyone arguing in the interests of a disputed dogma to insist on a literal interpretation of such peculiar forms of speech.

² The word *atonement* occurs in the New Testament but once, in the common English version of Rom. v, 11, where the Revised Version substitutes *reconciliation*. In the Old Testament it is the common rendering of some form of the Hebrew כפר, the primary meaning of which is to *cover*, as we have elsewhere explained. Hence as an English word it can have no weight in determining the biblical conception. *Propitiation* is a Latin term, and appears in the New Testament only as a translation of ἱλαστήριον in Rom. iii, 25, which we have shown to mean a *mercy seat* (as in Heb. ix, 5), and of ἱλασμός in 1 John ii, 2, and iv, 10. The word in these two last-named texts has obvious reference to what Christ does for the forgiveness and removal of the sins of the world, but furnishes no explanation of the *method* of the propitiation. *Expiation* is not a biblical word, and so far as it suggests anything other than what Scripture

inseparable from sacrificial customs and the ideas such customs were adapted to inculcate. These customs and ideas are also part and parcel of the religious history of mankind. We have aimed to indicate in the foregoing pages the fundamental ideas which attach to the Old Testament ritual of sacrifices and offerings, and also to guard the reader against pressing incidental points of analogy and symbolism too far. Language and illustrations based upon popular customs should always be treated as popular, not as exact and scientific in its purpose. To apprehend aright the vicarious element in the self-offering of Christ, we must eliminate the pagan notion of placating a wrathful Deity, and look more deeply into the spiritual significance of "the blood of Christ, who through the eternal Spirit offered himself without blemish unto God."

3. To make known a truth so far-reaching and profound, Christ and his apostles most fittingly appropriated figurative conceptions and forms of speech that were at once current and popular and sacredly associated with religious service. It is to be noted that our Lord chose the time of the passover for the laying down of his life in vicarious sacrifice, and that Paul speaks of the sacrifice of Christ as our passover (1 Cor. v, 7). Sacrificial worship, priestly intercession, and the lofty ideals of a covenant relation to God had furnished a large part of the providential preparation of the chosen people for

Use of current forms of speech.

---

teaches concerning atonement, propitiation, and reconciliation it has no place in a biblical theology.

NECESSITY OF MEDIATION. 181

the advent of the Christ. But the great prophets of Israel from Samuel onward had taught that sacrifices and burnt offerings were of no intrinsic value, and could not be acceptable before Jehovah unless expressive of a pure devotion of the heart of the worshiper and a faithful obedience to the word of God (comp. 1 Sam. xv, 22; Isa. i, 11-17; Hos. vi, 6; Mic. vi, 6-8; Amos v, 21-24; Jer. vi, 20; vii, 22, 23; Psa. xl, 6-8). Much more, then, may we suppose that our Lord and his apostles would penetrate beneath the forms of priestly service and of sacrifices (comp. Matt. xii, 5-8; 1 Cor. v, 7, 8; Rom. xii, 1, 2; Heb. ix, 9; x, 4), and fill their metaphorical allusions to them with the deepest spiritual significance. We should study in like manner to pass beyond the letter and to grasp the true spiritual import of such words as *atonement* and *propitiation* when applied to the sufferings of Christ. Our expositions, we trust, have shown that there is no need of loading the biblical writers with the pagan notions of placating a vengeful Deity, or of reconciling an offended God to the sinner. One may construct such a dogma, and many have so interpreted certain scattered texts of Scripture; but we think such a construction is unnecessary, and not justified in the light of the more authoritative statements of Christ and his apostles.

4. A certain divine necessity for the mediatorial sufferings of Christ is assumed in many scriptures (Matt. xvi, 21; xxvi, 54; Mark viii, 31; Luke ix, 22; xiii, 33; xvii, 25; Necessity of Christ's mediation.

xxii, 37; xxiv, 7, 26, 44, 46; John iii, 14; ix, 4; xii, 32-34; Acts iii, 18; iv, 12; xvii, 3; Heb. ix, 23); and aside from any such specific statement it would truly seem in the nature of things that such suffering and sacrifice must have been imperatively necessary or the only begotten Son of God would not thus have given up his life. Wherein, then, this necessity? Not, as we have read the Scriptures, in a demand of abstract justice to maintain God's honor and dignity as a Ruler of the moral world. God's righteousness, whether as Father, Ruler, or Judge, is sure to manifest itself in Love, so that even in the pardon of our sins and cleansing us from all unrighteousness he is ever "faithful and righteous" (1 John i, 9).

(1) The necessity for Christ's redeeming work is from our point of view most readily seen, first, in the sinfulness of man and his inability to release himself from its thraldom. The soul that sins must surely die (Gen. ii, 17; Ezek. xviii, 4, 20); "lust, when it hath conceived, beareth sin; and the sin, when it is full-grown, bringeth forth death" (James i, 15); "the wages of sin is death." When, therefore, we ask who shall deliver men from this fearful bondage of sin and of death our only answer is that such salvation is the free gift of God through Jesus Christ our Lord. It must come from above. There is no other way of life, no other name under heaven in whom we must be saved, if saved at all.[1]

Necessity in man.

---

[1] Studying the whole manifestation of God in Christ, we are

NECESSITY OF MEDIATION.

(2) But there is also intimation in such scriptures as John iii, 16, that there exist mysterious necessities in the nature of God, as well as in the helplessness of perishing men, that re- *Necessity in nature of God.* quired the giving of his only begotten Son to be the Saviour of the world. The creation of such a world as ours, with its myriad forms of life and its innumerable "offspring of God," capable of becoming children of God by heavenly birth and adoption, would seem to have involved obligations on the part of the Creator which no human mind can properly estimate. According to the profound conception of the Fourth Gospel, the Word that became flesh was with God in the entire process of creation, and no man has ever seen God or is capable of revealing him except "the only begotten Son, who is in the bosom of the Father." We may, accordingly, believe that, speaking after the manner of man, and not irreverently, the righteousness of love and the love of righteousness toward the dependent objects of his creation *God obligated by love.* required on the part of God a redemptive manifestation of himself in the mediation of Jesus Christ. We thus conceive God as the eternal Father counting himself obligated by every conceivable bond of love and righteousness to exert himself to the uttermost to save from sin and its perdition every creature whom he

---

led, especially in John's Gospel, to conceive him as light, life, love, righteousness, wisdom, power, and glory—a sevenfold revelation. Christ comes forth from the bosom of the Father, makes an end of the law for righteousness unto everyone that believeth, and brings life and immortality to light.

184   THE MEDIATION OF JESUS CHRIST.

permitted to come into being bearing the image and likeness of God. If, after all such mighty provisions of love, the human offspring persist in sin and "sell himself to do evil," the Father has proven his own unspeakable affection, and has discharged his own obligation.

5. The sufferings of Christ, then, are not to be thought of as a penalty. No righteousness, human or

Such suffering not penal. divine, can inflict penalty on the righteous or on any being that is not convicted of sin. But, according to Paul (Rom. viii, 3), "God, sending his own Son in the likeness of sinful flesh and concerning sin ($περὶ ἁμαρτίας$)[1] condemned sin in the flesh." The entire manifestation of Christ as the holy, self-sacrificing Son of God has broken the power of sin in human nature, and thus put it forever under condemning judgment (comp. 1 John iii, 8; Heb. ii, 14). And if we inquire further why Christ must suffer in this public condemnation of sin, the true answer is, because God suffers and must needs have suffered concerning sin as soon as it ever appeared in the moral world. Whatever view we take of Christ's life, work, and suffering, we must recognize in him some corresponding manifestation of his

---

[1] This phrase, being the usual rendering of the Hebrew for *sin offering* in the Septuagint (comp. Heb. x, 6, 8), may be explained in that sense here; or it may be explained as in substance equivalent to what this apostle expresses in somewhat stronger form in 2 Cor. v, 21. But it cannot be shown to mean that God visited *punishment* on Jesus Christ, as if by any sort of imputation he could be made a real substitute for the guilty and suffer the penalty due to them.

Father. And so when we behold Christ weeping and lamenting over Jerusalem, and crying, "O that thou hadst known the things that belong unto peace! How often would I have gathered thy children, but ye would not!" we behold the Father also. And in like manner in all his utterances of sorrow, of judgment, or of love he is the divinely anointed Revealer of the thoughts and feelings of God.

6. A fact not to be overlooked is that nothing which God in Christ has done or can do removes all consequences of sin. Sins that are past events, "the sins done beforetime," may be freely forgiven in the blessed forbearance of God, but they must forever remain as deeds of the past. They cannot possibly be undone, or cease to be facts in the history of the moral world. And the natural results or consequences of many sins work on through successive generations in spite of all the redeeming efficacy of the grace of God. These facts also serve to show that the great saving work of Christ is not to rescue man *from punishment* for wrongdoing, but rather to deliver him *from sin itself*. The sacrificial mediation of Christ is not a penalty for the sins of men, nor even a substitute for penalty; but it is rather to be apprehended as "a power of God unto salvation to every one that believeth." *[Does not remove all consequences of sin.]*

7. The biblical conception of Christ's work is not that of an objective process going on outside of humanity. Such a notion seems possible only as we are taught to think of the *[Not an objective process or ground.]*

atonement as "an objective ground" on which it is made possible for God to forgive sin. The logic of this conception implies that God's love and saving mercy could not be exercised *except as a result of Christ's offering his life as a ransom;* whereas, according to the Scripture, the entire mediation of Christ has its origin in the love of God. The sufferings of Christ are not the ground or cause of the exercise of God's saving grace; the love of God is the cause and source of the sufferings. So God is *in Christ,* not apart from Christ, reconciling the world unto himself. And the atonement, the propitiation, the reconcilation, is *in us, not apart from us.* Nor should we think of God as apart from his world, or outside of humanity, in any such way as to warrant our affirming objective grounds for his becoming reconciled to us.

8. It is evident, therefore, that we are to think of Christ's work of mediation as something essentially spiritual. Sacrifices and offerings have no value except as figures of spiritual realities, or as illustrations of heavenly truths. In his coming to do the will of God, and so to manifest the nature and power of God, Christ taketh away such formal rites that he may establish the will of the heavenly Father (Heb. x, 9). And it is the will of God that all men should be saved from sin. His love for the world has given his only begotten Son to reveal a saving grace sufficient to embrace all humanity. But the grace and the mediation can become

effective only as men in faith accept the heavenly provision and are born of the Spirit. Thus they "pass out of death into life," and "walk after the Spirit."

9. Inasmuch, then, as Christ's mediation is a spiritual work, it becomes effectual in the heart and life of men only as they become united with Christ by a strong living faith. *Effectual through a living faith.* The Christ of God is a living Saviour, and in him we have our most blessed access to God. The personal experiences of life and light and peace and fellowship with God enable the Christian believer to apprehend the profound significance of such biblical concepts as a personal participation in the sufferings of Christ (comp. Rom. viii, 17; 2 Cor. i, 5, 7; Phil. iii, 10; 1 Pet. iv, 13), a being crucified with Christ (Gal. ii, 20; v, 24; vi, 14; Rom. vi, 6), dying and being buried with Christ (Rom. vi, 4, 8; 2 Cor. v, 14; Col. ii, 12; iii, 3), and also rising and reigning with him (Eph. ii, 2; Col. ii, 12, 13; 2 Tim. ii, 11, 12). As we are thus "partakers of the sufferings of Christ" (1 Pet. iv, 13), we may also "become partakers of the divine nature" (2 Pet. i, 4). And so the conviction of sin, the deep sense of guilt, the experience of repentance and conversion, the remission of sin, the new birth from above, and all the blessedness of the new spiritual life "hid with Christ in God" are brought about by means of the redemption in Christ, and are possible in no other name under heaven or among men. Like the new birth *from above,* all these gracious experiences of salvation are opened unto us by reason of

the love and righteousness of God as revealed in the mediation of his Son Jesus Christ.

10. We offer no theory or philosophy of atonement in Christ other than what may appear in these state-
No theory of atonement. ments of the manifold Scripture teaching on the subject. The Scriptures certainly furnish us no theory of Christ's divine-human mediation, but we ought not therefore to condemn, as some do, all attempts to formulate such theories. For what is a theory of the atonement but an attempt to set forth a rational conception of the nature and necessity of Christ's redeeming work?[1] Regeneration and eternal life are impossible to man without the removal of his sinfulness and guilt, and the rational theorist inquires how this salvation is brought about in the manifestation of Christ. The result of our study has been to show that this divine redemptive mediation is so multifarious in its operation that no definitive theory can fairly express its depth and breadth and height. Whether we say with John iii, 16, "God so loved the world, that he gave his only begotten Son, that whoso-

---

[1] It would seem that each of the more notable theories of the atonement has had a sort of genetic relation to certain dominant ideas of the time when it originated. The patristic notion of a ransom paid to Satan for the release of mankind from his thrall could have been possible only at a time when crass doctrines of demonology were widely prevalent. The Anselmic theory of absolute satisfaction had a stronghold in mediæval ideas of absolute monarchy and the divine rights of kings. The "governmental theory" may be traced to Grotius and the prominence given in his day to international law. And the great humanitarian movements of the nineteenth century with their emphasis on altruism and moral reforms prepared the way for the "moral influence theory," and have supplied its chief arguments and illustrations.

No One Theory Sufficient. 189

ever believeth on him should not perish, but have eternal life;" or with 2 Cor. v, 19, "God was in Christ reconciling the world unto himself;" or with 1 Pet. iii, 18, "Christ suffered for sins once, the righteous for the sake of the unrighteous, that he might bring us to God;" or with 1 John iv, 10, "God loved us and sent his Son as a propitiation for our sins;" or with Heb. ii, 10, "It became God in bringing many sons unto glory, to make the author of their salvation perfect through sufferings"—whether, I say, we appropriate any one of these or of a score of other biblical statements of similar character and import, we express at most only an incomplete idea of all that belongs to Christ's mediation. The great work of redemption expressed in any one of these texts is generally found to be involved in one or more figures of speech which call for some measure of analysis and explanation. Hence appears the impossibility, also, of maintaining a doctrine of atonement in Christ on the basis of the language of divers texts of Scripture taken as so many authoritative utterances. A rational exegesis of each separate text and its immediate context often shows that men have read their doctrinal theories into biblical statements which furnish them no real support. While, therefore, a number and variety of observations may fairly summarize the teachings of Christ and his apostles on the subject, the doctrine of redemptive mediation in Jesus Christ is too broad and deep and mysterious to be satisfied with any single definition or theory.

11. There is, however, an ideal of "the mystical body of Christ," given in the New Testament, which

Mystical body of Christ.

should receive distinctive attention before we close this treatise on the divine-human mediation of our Lord. The profound truth of the communion of saints in and through the Spirit of Christ finds, perhaps, its most remarkable expression in John xvii, 20-26, where Jesus prays that all those, whom the divinely appointed ministry of reconciliation shall gather together out of the world, may be PERFECTED INTO ONE ($\tau\epsilon\tau\epsilon\lambda\epsilon\iota\omega\mu\acute{\epsilon}\nu o\iota$ $\epsilon\grave{\iota}\varsigma$ $\ddot{\epsilon}\nu$). They are all to be one, even as the Father is in the Son, and the Son is in the Father, that they may ultimately be with the glorified Christ in the heavenly light, and behold the glory and the love which were existent before the foundation of the world. There comes to us with these words an ideal of perfection in the love and fellowship of God which no comment of ours can place in clearer light. Paul's words about being raised up with Christ, and sitting "with him in the heavenlies" (Eph. ii, 6), seem like an echo of Jesus's intercessory prayer. "The heavenlies" of perfection in Christ and in God are not "heavenly places" merely, but heavenly fellowship of all saints, heavenly powers, heavenly wisdom and knowledge, and all heavenly glories of the life eternal.[1]

The vital unity of the mystical body of Christ is also shown in the figure of the vine and its branches (John xv, 1-9). Jesus is himself the genuine living vine, his

---

[1] See my *Biblical Hermeneutics*, p. 276. New York, 1890.

Father is the vinedresser, and his disciples are the branches which can have no fruit apart from the true vine. In strict accord with this ideal we are assured, in John vi, 53, that no one can possess the eternal life except he "eat the flesh of the Son of man and drink his blood." Thus only can the living Christ, "ascending up where he was before" (verse 62), bestow the heavenly manna, and make good the word, "He that eateth my flesh and drinketh my blood abideth in me, and I in him." These words are offensive to the literalist and the man of a carnal mind, but to the man of spiritual intuition they are instinct with spirit and with life. In the First Epistle of John (i, 3) we meet another statement of the same spiritual truth: "Our fellowship is with the Father, and with his Son Jesus Christ." Such fellowship is also called "abiding in the Son and in the Father," and constitutes the essence of "the life eternal" (ii, 24, 25).

The same rich mystical thought appears in Paul's allusions to the communion of saints at the Lord's table: "The cup of blessing which we bless, is it not a communion (κοινωνία, *a joint participation*) of the blood of Christ? The bread which we break, is it not a communion of the body of Christ?" (1 Cor. x, 16.) So again in 1 Cor. xii, 12, 13, we read: "As the body is one and hath many members, and all the members of the body, being many, are one body; so also is Christ. For in one Spirit were we all baptized into one body." The saints of all ages and lands are to be thus conceived as

Communion of saints.

constituting the mystical body of Christ, and they are "severally members thereof." They make up his "church, which is his body, the fullness of him that filleth all in all" (Eph. i, 23). This mystical body is not yet complete. Divers ministries of apostles and prophets and evangelists and pastors and teachers exist "for the perfecting of the saints, unto the building up of the body of Christ; till we all attain unto the unity of the faith, and of the knowledge of the Son of God, unto a full-grown man, unto the measure of the stature of the fullness of Christ" (Eph. iv, 12, 13). Here, surely, is an ideal of the great consummation contemplated in the mediation of Jesus Christ which inspires holiest thoughts. And when to all this we add the figure of the Church as the Spouse of Christ, who is at once her Saviour and her Lord, we but enhance our concept of the all-embracing love of God in Christ. The Lord Jesus is the Saviour of the mystical body, for he "loved the Church, and gave himself up for her, that he might present the Church to himself glorious, not having spot or wrinkle or any such thing" (Eph. v, 25-27). It is worthy of note that while in Pauline thought the Church of Christ was "purchased with his own blood" (Acts xx, 28), in the Apocalypse of John the great and glorious company of those who were, by the blood of the Lamb that was slain, "purchased for God out of every tribe, and tongue, and people, and nation" (v, 9), are shown in heavenly vision as "the Bride, the wife of the Lamb" (xxi, 9).

WITH THE LAMB AT THE THRONE. 193

This picture consummates our highest and final thought of "the redemption that is in Christ Jesus." By means of it we are elevated far above all special theories of the atonement. We "behold the Lamb of God, that taketh away the sin of the world." We behold the mystical body of Christ, all those who believe on him through the word of his apostles, sanctified and cleansed by the washing of water in the word, made one in the Father and in the Son, abiding in the heavenlies, and sharing in the glory of the risen and ascended Lord. The members of this mystical body are "a great multitude which no man can number, out of all peoples, arrayed in white robes, and palms in their hands, their robes washed and made white in the blood of the Lamb. *Therefore* are they before the throne of God, and he that sitteth on the throne shall spread his tabernacle over them, and the Lamb that is in the midst of the throne shall be their shepherd, and shall guide them unto fountains of waters of life: and God shall wipe away every tear from their eyes."

And thus we behold the Author of our salvation made perfect through sufferings, bringing many sons into glory, and saying, as he presents them in the presence of that glory with exceeding joy, "Behold, I and the children whom God hath given me." Thus we behold God, in Christ, through the eternal Spirit, reconciling the world unto himself.

INDEX.

THE NUMBERS INDICATE PAGES.

AGNI, 28.
Alford, 117.
Anselmic theory, 71, 188.
Anthropomorphism, 33.
Apis, 30.
Atonement, Day of, 42.
Avatar, 24.
Azazel, 47.

BARTH, 24.
Bhagavad Gita, 24.
Blood offerings, 44.
Brahmanism, 24.
Buddhism, 25.

CALVIN, 119.
Cereal offerings, 43.
Chinese ideas, 23.
Chrysostom, 119.
Clarke, 142.
Comforter, 88, 153, 175.
Conybeare, 117.
Copleston, 26.
Cremer, 119.
Cyril, 119.

DE WETTE, 117.
Dinkart, 23.
Dion Chrysostom, 117.
Dods, 158.

EGYPTIAN religion, 29.
Ellicott, 134.
Enoch, Book of, 47.

Erasmus, 119.
Erman, 29.

FEDERAL theology, 17.
Fetichism, 32.
Fire offerings, 46.
Frazer, 22.
Fritzsche, 117.

GIFFORD, 119.
Greek religion, 31.
Grotius, 119, 188.

HARDWICK, 29.
Hardy, 26.
Hare, 166.
Henotheism, 27.
Hinduism, 24.
Hodge, 117.
Hort, 73.
Horus, 30, 35.
Howson, 117.
Human sacrifices, 44.
Huther, 92.

IMMANENCE of God, 34.
Incarnation, 20.
Indra, 28.
Irenæus, 91.
Isis, 30.

JACKSON, 23.
Josephus, 118.
Jowett, 117.

KRISHNA, 30.
Kuyper, 155.

LANGE, 119.
Last supper, 72.
Latin mythology, 31.
Legge, 23.
Levitical priesthood, 40.
Liddon, 119.
Luther, 119.

MACKNIGHT, 141.
Mahan, 168.
Mazdian religion, 23.
Mercy seat, 112, 119-126.
Messianic hope, 64.
Meyer, 78, 117.
Moberly, 159.
Muller, 27.
Mystery of ages, 17, 66.

NIRVANA, 25.
Nonnus, 117.

ODYSSEY, 31.
Olshausen, 119.
Origen, 119.
Osiris, 30.

PARACLETE, 88, 153.
Penitential psalms, 61.
Philippi, 119, 128.
Polytheism, 32.
Priest Codex, 43.
Purpose of ages, 17.

RECONCILIATION to God, 102-104, 130.
Rig-Veda, 27.
Ritschl, 119.

SACRIFICES, 42.
Schaff, 125.
Sin offering, 46.
Stevens, 18.
Supper, Last, 72.
Swete, 117.

TELEOLOGY, 19.
Theodoret, 119, 125.
Theophylact, 119.
Tholuck, 119.
Totemism, 32.
Transmigration, 25.
Trespass offering, 45.

UMBREIT, 119.

VARUNA, 27.
Veda, 26.
Vishnu, 24, 35.
Vohuman, 23.

WESTCOTT, 73, 144, 146, 148.
Whedon, 174.
Wiedemann, 30.
Williams, 26.
Wordsworth, 117.

ZEUS, 31.
Zoroaster, 23.

APPENDIX
A SELECT BIBLIOGRAPHY

A SELECT BIBLIOGRAPHY

FOR THE CONVENIENCE AND USE OF
SPECIAL STUDENTS IN

BIBLICAL THEOLOGY AND BIBLICAL DOGMATICS.

So far as satisfactory English translations exist the original titles are not given.

ADENEY, WALTER F.—The Theology of the New Testament. New York, 1894.
A brief, readable, and useful compendium.

ALEXANDER, W. LINDSAY.—A System of Biblical Theology. 2 vols. Edinburgh, 1888.
Consists of theological lectures, abridged, arranged, and edited from the author's manuscripts by James Ross. Is comprehensive, and combines some features of both biblical and systematic theology.

BAUMGARTEN-CRUSIUS, L. F. O.—Grudzüge der biblischen Theologie. Jena, 1828.
Interesting mainly as one of the earlier efforts to construct a biblical rather than a confessional theology.

BAUER, GEORG LORENZ.—Theologie des alten Testaments, oder Abriss der religiösen Begriffe der alten Hebräer, von den ältesten Zeiten bis auf den Anfang der christlichen Epoche. Leipzig, 1796.

....Biblische Theologie des neuen Testaments. 4 vols. Leipzig, 1800-1802.
Valuable for studying the early attempts to distinguish Old and New Testament theology, and to note the various types of doctrine in the different biblical writers.

BAUR, FERDINAND CHRISTIAN.—Vorlesungen über die neutestamentliche Theologie. Leipzig, 1864. New edition with Introduction by Otto Pfleiderer. Gotha, 1892.
These lectures were first edited by F. F. Baur, son of the author. They give the distinguished professor's views on the teaching of Christ and of the apostles more fully than any one of his other works.

BECK, J. T.—Vorlesungen über christliche Glaubenslehre. 2 vols. Ed. by Lindenmeyer. Gütersloh, 1886-1887.
The second volume gives under four main sections a valuable outline of biblical dogmatics.

BERNARD, THOMAS D.—The Progress of Doctrine in the New Testament. New York, 1867. New ed., 1900.
The Bampton Lectures for 1864, and worthy of note as an early English attempt at biblical theology.

BEYSCHLAG, WILLIBALD.—New Testament Theology, or Historical Account of the Teaching of Jesus and of Primitive Christianity according to the New Testament Sources. English Translation by Neil Buchanan. 2 vols. Edinburgh, 1894.
The most able and commanding work on New Testament theology that is now accessible to English readers. No student in this department can afford to do without it.

BIEDERMANN, ALOIS E.—Christliche Dogmatik. 2 vols. Berlin, 1884-1885.
The first 169 pages of the second volume, under the title of *Die Schriftlehre*, contains a valuable outline of biblical dogmatics.

BOVON, J.—Théologie du Nouveau Testament. 2 vols. Lausanne, 1893-1894.
In this learned and valuable treatise the New Testament is recognized as the historical foundation and beginning of the author's proposed " Study of the Work of Redemption." The first volume discusses the life and teaching of Jesus, and the second presents the apostolic teaching under five sections: (1) Jewish Christianity, (2) Paulinism, to which the Epistle to the Hebrews belongs as "Paulinism of the second degree," (3) the Catholic Epistles, (4) the Apocalypse, and (5) the Johannine Theology.

BRUCE, ALEXANDER BELMAIN.—The Kingdom of God; or, Christ's Teaching according to the Synoptic Gospels. Edinburgh, 1890.

....St. Paul's Conception of Christianity. New York, 1894.

....The Epistle to the Hebrews. The First Apology for Christianity. Edinburgh and New York, 1899.
These, like all the works of Professor Bruce, are of permanent value, and deserve repeated study.

BUESCHING, A. F.—Dissertatio exhibens epitomen theologiæ e solis literis sanctis concinnatæ. Göttingen, 1756.
Deserving notice chiefly as one of the very earliest efforts to construct a biblical rather than a dogmatic and scholastic theology.

BIBLIOGRAPHY. 201

COELLN, DANIEL GEORG CONRAD VON.—Biblische Theologie, mit einer Nachricht über des Verfassers Leben und Wirken, herausgegeben von David Schulz. 2 vols. Leipzig, 1836.
Exhibits extensive learning, but follows the method of De Wette and adopts his headings for the main divisions. The Old Testament theology is given under the two heads of Hebraism and Judaism, and that of the New Testament under (1) The Teaching of Jesus, and (2) The Teaching of the Apostles.

CONE, ORELLO.—The Gospel and its Earliest Interpreters. New York, 1893.
A suggestive work, well worthy of attention.

CRAMER, L. D.—Vorlesungen über die biblischen Theologie des neuen Testaments. Edited by Næbe. Leipzig, 1830.

CREMER, AUGUST H.—Biblisch-theologisches Wörterbuch der neutestamentlichen Gräcität. Gotha, 1866. Many later editions. English Translation by William Urwick. Edinburgh, 1872. Several later editions.
An invaluable work, indispensable to the scientific student of New Testament theology.

DE WETTE, WILHELM MARTIN LEBERECHT.—Biblische Dogmatik des alten und neuen Testaments; oder kritische Darstellung der Religionslehre des Hebraismus, des Judenthums und Urchristenthums. Berlin, 1813. Third improved edition, 1831.
Like all the productions of this author, a masterpiece of lucid, concise, and comprehensive presentation of the subjects which it handles. The first and larger part of the volume sets forth the religion of the Old Testament under the heads of Hebraism and Judaism. The apocryphal books, Philo, and Josephus are drawn upon as sources of information, as well as the canonical books. The New Testament part treats the teaching of Jesus and that of the apostles under two distinct divisions,

DILLMANN, AUGUST.—Handbuch der alttestamentlichen Theologie. Herausgegeben von R. Kittel. Leipzig, 1895.
Accurate in its statements, thorough in exegesis, and always helpful.

DRUMMOND, ROBERT J.—The Relation of the Apostolic Teaching to the Teaching of Christ. Edinburgh, 1900.
The Kerr Lectures for 1900. Somewhat discursive, but contains much of real worth.

DUFF, ARCHIBALD.—Old Testament Theology; or, The History of Hebrew Religion from the Year 800 B. C. London, 1891.
This volume deals mainly with the books of Amos, Micah, and portions of Isaiah, and furnishes much valuable material for the study of Old Testament theology.

202 BIBLIOGRAPHY.

DUHM, BERNHARD.—Die Theologie der Propheten, als Grundlage für die innere Entwicklungsgeschichte der israelitischen Religion. Bonn, 1875.
A valuable help in tracing the historical development of biblical doctrines in the prophets of the different periods of Assyrian, Babylonian, and Persian supremacy.

EVERETT, C. C.—The Gospel of Paul. Boston, 1893.

ESTES, DAVID FOSTER.—An Outline of New Testament Theology. Boston, 1900.

EWALD, HEINRICH.—Old and New Testament Theology. English Translation by T. Goadby. Edinburgh, 1888.
Ewald's German work consists of four volumes and covers a wide field. This translation is confined mainly to the second and third volumes, and treats of God and the universe, the nature of faith in Christ, the Christian Trinity, and immortality.

FULLIQUET, GEORGES.—La Pensée religieuse dans le Nouveau Testament. Étude de Théologie Biblique. Paris, 1894.
A popular and interesting exposition of New Testament doctrine, with special emphasis on the relation of doctrines to spiritual life and experience.

GOULD, EZRA P.—The Biblical Theology of the New Testament. New York, 1900.
An admirable treatise in small compass, but quite comprehensive in its plan and method.

HAUPT, ERICH.—Die eschatologischen Aussagen Jesu in den synoptischen Evangelien. Berlin, 1895.

HITZIG, FERDINAND.—Vorlesungen über biblische Theologie und messianische Weissagungen des alten Testaments. Herausgegeben von Kneucker. Karlsruhe, 1880.
Apparently lacking in unity of aim and in comprehensiveness, but, like all this author's works, incisive, suggestive, and critical.

HOFMANN, JOHANN CHR. KARL VON.—Der Schriftbeweis. Ein theologischer Versuch. 2 vols. Nördlingen, 1852–1856. 2d ed., 1857–1860. (2d vol. in two large parts.)

....Biblische Theologie des neuen Testaments. Nach Manuskripten und Vorlesungen bearbeitet von W. Volck. Nördlingen, 1886.
The older work is a mine of valuable exegetical discussions of biblical doctrine, and has exerted wide influence on subsequent writers The later work, edited by Volck, is an excellent compendium of New Testament theology.

HOLSTEN, KARL JOHANN.—Zum Evangelium des Paulus und des Petrus. Rostock, 1867.

....Das Evangelium des Paulus dargestellt. Berlin, 1880.

....Paulinische Theologie dargestellt. Berlin, 1898.

Valuable as the successive contributions of one who was a leader in the formulation of Pauline theology.

HOLTZMANN, HEINRICH JULIUS.—Lehrbuch der neutestamentlichen Theologie. 2 vols. Leipzig, 1897.

Somewhat radical in its critical treatment of the documentary sources of New Testament theology, but easily to be ranked among the most thorough, scientific, comprehensive, and masterly works on the subject extant.

HORTON, R. F.—The Teaching of Jesus, London, 1896.

IMMER, A.—Theologie des neuen Testaments. Bern, 1877.

This learned and comprehensive treatise discusses (1) the Religion of Jesus; (2) the Jewish Christianity of the primitive apostles; (3) Paulinism; (4) the post-Pauline Jewish Christianity; (5) the mediating course between Paulinism and Jewish Christianity; and (6) the Johannine Gospel and First Epistle.

KAYSER, AUGUST.—Die Theologie des alten Testaments, in ihrer geschichtlichen Entwicklung dargestellt. Nach des Verfassers Tode herausgegeben mit einem Vorwort von Ed. Reuss. Strassburg, 1886.

KNAPP, GEORGE CHRISTIAN.—Lectures on Christian Theology, translated by Leonard Woods. 2 vols. Andover, 1831-1832. 8th American ed. 1 vol. New York, 1859.

An elaborate work of real value. It is cast in the form of a systematic theology, but is, in fact, a very full treatise on biblical dogmatics. In its English translation it has had an extensive circulation.

KROP, FREDERIC.—La Pensée de Jésus sur le Royaume de Dieu d'après les Évangiles synoptiques avec un appendice sur la question du "Fils de l'homme." Paris, 1897.

LADD, GEORGE T.—The Doctrine of Sacred Scripture. A critical, historical, and dogmatic Inquiry into the origin and nature of the Old and New Testaments. 2 vols. New York, 1883.

An exceedingly valuable work, but too diffusely written to serve the most helpful purpose. It treats many of the most important topics of biblical doctrine, and is a storehouse of information.

LAIDLAW, JOHN.—The Bible Doctrine of Man; or, The Anthropology and Psychology of Scripture. Edinburgh, 1879. New ed., 1895.

Belongs strictly to works on biblical dogmatics, and is well worthy of thoughtful study.

LUTZ, J. L. S.—Biblische Dogmatik. Nach dessen Tode herausgegeben von Rudolf Rutschi, mit einem Vorwort von Schneckenburger. Pforzheim, 1847.
A comprehensive and valuable contribution for its time.

MÉNÉGOZ, EUGÈNE.—Le Péche et la Redemption d'après Saint Paul. Paris, 1882.

....La Predestination dans la Théologie Paulinienne. Paris, 1884.

....La Théologie de l'Épitre aux Hébreaux. Paris, 1894.
These are all treatises of sterling value.

MILLIGEN, GEORGE.—The Theology of the Epistle to the Hebrews, with a critical Introduction. Edinburgh, 1899.
A volume to be cordially commended to students.

MOORHOUSE, J.—The Teaching of Christ: its Conditions, Secret, and Results. London, 1891.

NEANDER, JOHANN AUGUST W.—History of the Planting and Training of the Christian Church by the Apostles. Translated by J. E. Ryland. Revised by E. G. Robinson. New York, 1865.
An old standard work, having permanent value for the student of New Testament theology.

NOACH, LUDWIG.—Die biblische Theologie. Einleitung in's alte und neue Testament, und Darstellung des Lehrgehaltes der biblischen Bücher nach ihrer Entstehung und ihrem geschichtlichen Verhältniss. Halle, 1853.
Treats the Old and New Testament in two parts, but bestows much more attention to the literature than to the doctrinal contents.

OEHLER, G. F.—Theology of the Old Testament. A revision of the translation in Clark's Foreign Theological Library, with additions of the second German edition, an Introduction and Notes by George E. Day. New York, 1883.
A comprehensive and standard work, arranged under the three heads of Mosaism, Prophetism, and Old Testament Wisdom.

PFLEIDERER, OTTO.—Der Paulinismus. Leipzig, 1873. 2d ed., 1890.

....Paulinism: a Contribution to the History of Primitive Theology. Translated by Edward Peters. 2 vols. London, 1877.

....The Influence of the Apostle Paul on the Development of Christianity. Translated by J. F. Smith. New York, 1855.
All these works are indispensable to the critical study of New Testament theology, but the author's views are often radical, and have not met with general favor.

BIBLIOGRAPHY. 205

PIEPENBRING, CH.—Theology of the Old Testament. Translated from the French by H. G. Mitchell. New York, 1893.
Exhibits the development of religious thought among the Hebrew people.

RIEHM, EDWARD KARL AUGUST.—Der Lehrbegriff des Hebräerbriefes dargestellt und mit verwandten Lehrbegriffen verglichen. Basel. In two parts, 1858-1859. New and improved ed. in one vol., 1867.
An elaborate and masterly exposition of the doctrines of the Epistle to the Hebrews, along with comparison with corresponding ideas in the other biblical writers.

RITSCHL, ALBRECHT.—Die christliche Lehre von der Rechtfertigung und Versöhnung. 3 vols. Bonn, 1870-1874.
The second volume of this famous work (2d ed., 1882) treats the "biblical material of the doctrine," and is an important contribution to biblical theology. The influence of Ritschl on the modern theological thought of Germany has been powerful and far-reaching, and is now felt in much of the English world.

SABATIER, A.—The Apostle Paul. A Sketch of the Development of his Doctrine. Translated by A. M. Hellier. Edited, with an additional Essay on the Pastoral Epistles, by George G. Findlay. 3d ed. New York, 1896.
An important contribution to the Pauline theology.

SCHLOTTMANN, KONSTANTIN.—Compendium der biblischen Theologie des alten und neuen Testaments. Herausgegeben von Ernst Kühn. Leipzig, 1889. 2d ed., 1895.
A very convenient and comprehensive manual, covering both the Old and the New Testament.

SCHMID, CHRISTIAN FRIEDRICH.—Biblical Theology of the New Testament. Translated by G. H. Venables. Edinburgh, 1871.
One of the earlier and best-known books on the subject, and still worthy of consultation.

SCHMIDT, WILHELM.—Die Lehre des Apostels Paulus. Gütersloh, 1898.
Critical, and deserving the attention of students in Pauline theology.

SCHNEDERMANN, GEORG.—Jesu Verkündigung und Lehre vom Reiche Gottes in ihrer geschichtlichen Bedeutung. Erste Hälfte: Die Verkündigung Jesu vom Kommen des Königsreiches Gottes. Leipzig, 1893.

SCHULTZ, HERMANN.—Old Testament Theology. The Religion of Revelation in its pre-Christian Stage and Development. Translated from the fourth German edition by J. A. Paterson. 2 vols. Edinburgh, 1892.

The learned and accomplished author modified his critical views of Old Testament literature and doctrine after his first German edition of this work was issued (1869), and his more matured opinions appear in this translation (made from the 4th German ed.). It holds a commanding place among works on Old Testament theology.

SEEBERG, ALFRED.—Der Tod Christi in seiner Bedeutung für die Erlösung. Eine biblisch-theologische Untersuchung. Leipzig, 1895.

A remarkably comprehensive discussion of the saving significance of the death of Christ, and an important contribution to biblical theology; but not altogether satisfactory. It maintains the essential harmony of all the New Testament writers in their views of Christ's death, but he begins with the Epistle to the Hebrews, and then examines, in order, the teaching of John, of Paul, of Peter, the speeches recorded in the Acts, and, last of all, the Synoptic Gospels.

SOMERVILLE, DAVID.—St. Paul's Conception of Christ; or, The Doctrine of the Second Adam. Edinburgh, 1897.

A book that cannot well be overlooked in the study of Paul's Christology.

STEUDEL, JOH. CHRISTIAN FRIEDRICH.—Vorlesungen über die Theologie des alten Testamentes. Nach dessen Tode herausgegeben von G. F. Oehler. Berlin, 1840.

One of the older books that deserves study. It adopts the method of biblical dogmatics in three parts: (1) the Doctrine of Man, (2) the Doctrine of God, and (3) the Doctrine of the Relation between God and Man.

STEVENS, GEORGE B.—The Theology of the New Testament. New York, 1899.

....The Pauline Theology: a Study of the Origin and Correlation of the doctrinal teaching of the Apostle Paul. New York, 1892.

....The Johannine Theology: a Study of the doctrinal contents of the Gospel and Epistles of the Apostle John. New York, 1894.

These volumes constitute the most important and valuable contribution which American scholarship has thus far made to biblical theology. They all deserve cordial recommendation to students of New Testament doctrine.

BIBLIOGRAPHY. 207

TITIUS, ARTHUR.—Jesu Lehre vom Reiche Gottes. Freiburg. 1895.

A very thorough and systematic statement of the doctrine of the kingdom of God, and worthy of special commendation.

VAN OOSTERZEE, J. J.—The Theology of the New Testament. A Handbook for Bible Students. Translated from the Dutch by M. J. Evans. New York, 1871.

A condensed, convenient, and useful manual.

VATKE, WILHELM.—Die biblische Theologie wissenschaftlich dargestellt. Die Religion des alten Testamentes, nach den kanonischen Büchern entwickelt. Erster Theil. Berlin, 1835.

This first part is devoted to a presentation of the religion of the Old Testament, and the work was never completed by a further setting forth of the theology of the other canonical books. This work is noted as one of the first attempts to construct the historical development of the Old Testament theology after the manner now generally adopted by the more advanced biblical criticism.

WEISS, BERNHARD.—Biblical Theology of the New Testament. Translated from the third German edition by David Eaton. 2 vols. Edinburgh, 1882.

A work of exceeding value and a thesaurus of material for working out the problems of New Testament doctrine. It ranks among the foremost of its class.

WEISS, JOHANNIS.—Die Predigt vom Reiche Gottes. Göttingen, 1892. 2d ed., 1900.

....Die Idee des Reiches Gottes in der Theologie. Giessen, 1901.

The last named was read at a theological conference at Giessen, and is a supplement to the preceding. They both maintain the eschatological conception of the kingdom of God.

WENDT, HANS HINRICH.—The Teaching of Jesus. Translated by John Wilson. New York, 1892.

This English translation gives only the second part of the German original, but it contains the author's exposition of the teaching of Jesus. The first part is a critical discussion of the Gospels as sources of doctrine. A second edition of the German work (Göttingen, 1901) has condensed the two volumes of the first edition into one of 640 pages. No other work on the teaching of our Lord holds a higher place among New Testament scholars.

WITTICHEN, CARL.—Beiträge zur biblischen Theologie:

....1. Die Idee Gottes als des Vaters; ein Beitrag zur biblischen Theologie, hauptsächlich der synoptischen Reden Jesu. Göttingen, 1865.

....2. Die Idee des Menschen, zweiter Beitrag zur biblischen Theologie hauptsächlich der synoptischen Reden Jesu. Göttingen, 1868.

....3. Die Idee des Reiches Gottes, dritter Beitrag zur biblischen Theologie, inbesondere der synoptischen Reden Jesu. Göttingen, 1872.

These three small volumes present altogether an admirable outline and discussion of the biblical doctrine of the Father, of Man, and of the Kingdom of God. While dealing mainly with the teaching of Jesus, they also pay becoming attention to the other biblical writings, especially the Old Testament and the Apocrypha.

ZACHARIÄ, GOTTHILF TRAUGOTT.—Biblische Theologie, oder Untersuchung des Grundes der vornehmsten biblischen Lehren. 4 vols. Göttingen, 1771–1775.

Interesting as one of the elaborate treatises of its time, and one of the early attempts at biblical theology, but of little value for a modern student.

www.ingramcontent.com/pod-product-compliance
Lightning Source LLC
Chambersburg PA
CBHW071442150426
43191CB00008B/1203